Colleen,

You, me & Cross

Professor Mulrooney!!

Thanks for the support

D0016764

What they're saying about *ProActive Selling* and "the Tools"...

"Skip Miller of M3, with his ProActive Selling tools and methodologies, has been instrumental in changing a hardware-oriented sales culture at McData into a solutions-led sales team that engages our customers in a business based dialog."
  —**Gary Gysin,** Senior VP, WW Sales and Service, McData

"ProActive Selling has equipped our sales team with tools that set them apart from the competition, help to create strategic partnerships with our prospects and customers, win deals, and make our sales team BIG MONEY $$$$! We love it! No other sales tools have proven as effective or compelling"
  —**Victoria Rose,** VP Sales, NSB Corporation

"Our entire sales management team read *ProActive Selling* and attended ProActive Sales Management classes. The tools we learned from Skip Miller have given us the metrics and accountability tools that helped to drive us to record sales and profits this past year! We can't wait for Skip's next book!"
  —**Andrew G. Larson,** President & CEO, Gustave A. Larson Company

"I have read *ProActive Sales Management,* and without a doubt the tools will help you hire better and manage performance more effectively."
  —**Mike Daily,** VP Sales, Right90

Other Books by Skip Miller

Knock Your Socks Off Prospecting

ProActive Selling

ProActive Sales Management

Ultimate Sales Tool Kit

Ultimate Sales Tool Kit

The Versatile 15-Piece Set That
Every Professional Needs

Skip Miller

AMACOM
American Management Association
New York • Atlanta • Brussels • Chicago • Mexico City • San Francisco
• Shanghai • Tokyo • Toronto • Washington, D. C.

Special discounts on bulk quantities of AMACOM books are available to corporations, professional associations, and other organizations. For details, contact Special Sales Department, AMACOM, a division of American Management Association, 1601 Broadway, New York, NY 10019.
Tel.: 212-903-8316. Fax: 212-903-8083.
Website: www. amacombooks.org

This publication is designed to provide accurate and authoritative information in regard to the subject matter covered. It is sold with the understanding that the publisher is not engaged in rendering legal, accounting, or other professional service. If legal advice or other expert assistance is required, the services of a competent professional person should be sought.

Library of Congress Cataloging-in-Publication Data

Miller, William, 1955–
    Ultimate sales tool kit: the versatile 15-piece set that every professional needs / Skip Miller.
        p. cm.
    Includes bibliography references and index.
    ISBN-13: 978-0-8144-7400-6 (alk. paper)
    ISBN-10: 0-8144-7400-4 (alk. paper)
    1. Selling. 2. Success in business. I. Title.

    HF5438.25.M568 2007
    658.85—dc22   2006030259

Printing number
10 9 8 7 6 5 4 3 2 1

C O N T E N T S

PART 1
The Beginning

PART 2
The Middle

PART **3**

The End

ACKNOWLEDGMENTS

Once again, the people at AMACOM and AMA are just unbelievable. Thanks to Christina, Ellen, Hank, Heather, Matt, and Arlene. The world would be a lot less effective without all these sales tools, and your help to bring them to market.

To the customers who keep writing me and telling me how these tools work, even after years of learning about them: Don, Keith, Kevin, Dan, Jewell, Dave, Mike, Victoria, Gary, Bob, Steve.... The list goes on and on. Thank you for you help and support.

To my friends, who in spite of my travels and weird schedules, still offer support and help: Kim, Tim, Pat, Ron, Steve, Jon, Michael, Rob, Colon, Russ, Don.... Thanks.

Family, you know who you are. Thanks...all 55 of ya.

Kyle, you have impressed me every day. You are the definition of the word "leader." Alex, you are turning out to be quite a woman, and a darling to all who know you. Keep that spirit alive. Brianna, your empathy and love for all are famous. You are a special, special person. I am blessed to have such great kids.

Susan...to the love of my life.

To Dance or Not to Dance...

You have been there. And you know what to do. We have all been there. It's that crucial time: The sale is yours for the taking. You can feel it. It's time to use your experience from all those years of selling. It's time to use those tools you have used in the past, since they have worked so well for you before. It's time for you to grab the spotlight, take a deep breath...and dance.

...and when a major sale is on the line, boy can you dance.

Dancing is very effective, but there has to be a better way of making sales calls. I have observed salespeople for more than 10 years, and my observations about salespeople and how they perform on sales calls are:

1. Most salespeople use "sales success patterns" on their sales calls. I call these success patterns tools.

2. Salespeople have an average of three success patterns, or tools, at their disposal.

1

3. Tools are usually thought up and applied during a sales call in reaction to something a prospect says or does. This is also known as the "a great idea that just came to me" method.

4. Salespeople rarely practice tools. They prefer winging it, or using whatever tool comes to them during the sales call.

5. Most salespeople add a new tool to their tool kit less than once a year. Can you imagine any other profession—doctor, lawyer, or firefighter, for example— saying they rarely add new tools to their tool kits? A doctor who won't learn about a new drug, a lawyer a new law, a firefighter a new piece of equipment?

Salespeople get stuck in their ways, it seems. They measure their success by how they do against quota, then go back out and do the same things again. Oh sure, they subscribe to the theory, "What's good enough to have gotten you where you are today is not good enough to get you to where you need to be tomorrow." And yet they think sales training is analogous to a lobotomy. Salespeople would rather plug away with the few tools they have than spend time getting good at new ones.

> **Insanity:** doing the same thing over and over again and expecting different results.

Who could blame them? Most sales training asks you to swallow the whole thing, give up what you are doing, and change the way you sell. Not too many salespeople want to give up their success patterns. But the market is changing. Your customers are changing. So are your products. How your customers are buying, as well as what you are selling, is different than it was even 12 months ago. Decisions are being made faster; customers are more demanding. And because you're still using your tools from a few years ago, it's all coming down to price.

> If all things are equal, a deal will come down to price.
> But if all things are equal, why do we need salespeople?
> It's a salesperson's job to create and sustain a value
> difference.

YOU'RE WINGING IT, AREN'T YOU?

Selling can be a very rewarding career. It's a great profession. To be successful, salespeople have to be on their game every day. You never know when an opportunity is going to present itself, and great salespeople know being prepared is half the battle. It's rewarding because you get as much back as you decide to put into it.

One problem salespeople face is going into a sale thinking they are prepared. They believe that their years of experience or the exhaustive training they endured will help them on their sales calls. Sure, their experience and training will help them, but it will also limit them, since they will only use sales tactics or tools they can remember.

> That sales training was about a year ago, and the book is
> back on the shelf.... It's really a good-looking book,
> too.... Can't really remember too much...had a good
> time though....

In addition, at important times during the call, salespeople will only use tools they are good at or have confidence in. But they won't use the right tool for the right situation.

Imagine a handyman—let's call him Tim—on the job with

only a hammer and a drill. Tim does a great job. He's a hammer and drill expert. He has used these tools on almost every job he has gone on in the past five years. Obviously, he knows how to use them better than most.

One day Tim comes across a job that requires him to use other tools, maybe a screwdriver or a wrench. Tim knows those tools; heck, he bought some good ones too, but he uses them infrequently. As a matter of fact, Tim keeps those tools back at the shop. Why bring all those "extra" tools that he will never use on a job? So Tim gets out his hammer and drill and somehow he finds a way to make them work and get the job done.

Tim got lucky.

Tim needs to get better.

Tim needs to get good.

For Tim to get good, really good, he needs to bring more tools to the job site. He has worked with screwdrivers, pliers, and wrenches before. In this case, however, he just didn't have the right tool for the right job at the right time.

The *Ultimate Sales Tool Kit* gives every salesperson an array of tools for every sales call. Use it as a quick reference so you can grab the right tool at the right time on every call.

Moreover, the *Tool Kit* is a quick review, so any salesperson can have a set of instructions that she or he can reference whenever there is a need for a quick refresher on how to use a particular tool.

The 16 sales tools in this tool kit will allow you to:

* Be prepared

* Have the right tool at the right time

* Use all your skills, not just the ones you are good at or used that last time

- Help with sales call structure
- Have a powerful way to close every call
- Talk with decision makers in their language
- Get prospects to call you back
- Ask the right questions quickly to qualify a sale

Bottom line: you need more tools in your toolbox, not more of the same and not necessarily better ones than what you already have. After all, the ones you are using today have made you successful. There's no need to mess with them. We're talking about adding new tools that you can leverage every day, tools you can use at the point of attack—the sales call.

There are tools here for every part of a sales call: prospecting, education, transfer of ownership, the proposal, and the decision. But you will never use all the tools in the *Tool Kit* on a single sales call. The art of selling involves choosing the right tool at the right time.

HOW THIS BOOK WORKS

Knowing What to Do. In sales, knowing what to do is easy. Either you already know what to do or your boss tells you— or perhaps marketing or product management tells you. You listen, you agree; then if you can remember what it was, you do it.

Knowing How to Do It. How to do it is another matter: how to execute a sales call so that it is mutually beneficial to both parties; how to stay in control of the sale without making the prospect feel he's being "sold to." How is richer, deeper, and more challenging than what.

Inside this Tool Kit, you'll find tools to help you with the "what" as well as the "how" of selling, which makes it the perfect handbook for you to use. These are tools you can learn to use and put in your tool kit so you'll be prepared for those crucial moments during a sales call; tools you can practice with and get so good at that when it comes time to dance, you'll know more than just waltz or hip-hop.

The Rules

The rules of this book are simple—and yes, there are rules. The first, and primary, rule is:

"Fly balls get caught."
—**Gary Berman,** baseball coach

It's a simple rule. When up at bat, your little league son or daughter wants to hit one out of the park. You know the fence is too far back...fly balls get caught.

It is more effective to hit the ball hard, either on the ground or on a line, than to hit a deep fly ball that is going to get caught. It is a simple tool or rule that the player can use every time at bat, just like you. Sure, you want to make a sale on every sales call, and home runs look great. But by doing the things that give you the highest probability of success, you will win more games, period.

Rule 2: Each tool in the *Tool Kit* is covered in its own chapter with an explanation and examples. Each tool also has a unique Visual Exercise Area (VEA) to remind you of the tool and to make a quick reference point to help you remember not only what to do on a sales call but how to do it. If you really want to get better at sales, you must do the Visual Exercise Areas. If you read this book without doing the VEAs, you'll be able to say:

"Hey, this is a pretty cool book."

And it is. But it's even cooler to acquire the tools for your own sales tool kit. Please do the VEAs at the end of each tool chapter, so you can say:

"Hey, I'm getting better."

If you want the VEAs in electronic format, you can download them for free at www.m3learning.com.

The Structure

The Ultimate Sales Tool Kit is divided into three major areas.

* **Beginning:** Tools for prospecting and the early part of a sale

* **Middle:** Tools in the education and transfer of ownership steps

* **End:** Tools for closing a sale

This is your book. Feel free to highlight, circle, and draw on the pages. Do whatever it takes to make sure you understand the tool and its use.

Take It on Your Sales Calls

These are tools to be used when you are at bat, during the sales call, so keep the book handy. You should even feel comfortable taking your tool kit on sales calls and practicing your tactics before the call. Think of it as a guide, like a dictionary for a writer or a *Fodor's Travel Guide* for a tourist. Reference it often. Use the tools every day.

The Process^{Tool}

THE TOOLBOX—KIM AND TIM

Kim needed to finish his home repair job by the end of the day. He looked at the job one more time. It was slow going.

He decided he'd better get some help. His neighbor, Tim the Handyman, had a garage full of tools. If anyone knew of a quicker way to get a job done, it was Tim.

When Kim called for help, Tim came right over. After taking one look at the job, he ran back home and returned with his big red tool kit.

In a matter of minutes, Tim selected the tools he would need. And just a few hours later, he was finished—the project was complete. Tim hadn't needed all his tools, just the right ones for the job.

How many times have you said to yourself after a sales call: "Oh, now I get it! I know exactly what the prospect wanted. Why didn't I say...?"

Because you didn't get to the right tool at the right time!
Believe it or not, Kim actually had the right tools in his garage.
But they were scattered about and he couldn't get to them. He
needed a place to store them, a place where he could reach them.
Kim needed a tool kit.

If you're serious about using the tools in this book, you'll
need to understand how buyers buy, not just how salespeople sell.
Here are the steps of a buy process.

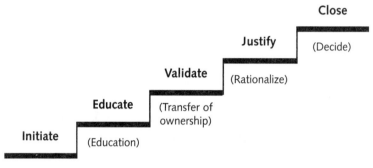

Prospects buy in a process. They really do. Think about it. For
prospects to get involved with a seller, they have to have an *initial interest*. They need their interest level excited, so once interested, they are ready to learn more, or go to *education.*

As a second step, prospects need and want to be educated.
This of course implies two-way education, where the prospect
dives in and tries to learn everything he can about what he is purchasing, and the salesperson educates himself about the prospect,
too.

Once prospects have been educated, they need to *validate*
their decision. They need to take ownership of the reason they are
making this change. They try the shoes on, test drive the car, agree
to a 30-day trial, or take a sample. Once their decision has been
validated to their satisfaction, they *rationalize* their decision. This

is where they come up with a few more questions—you know them as objections—that need to be addressed, or they will not go any further along in their process.

Finally, once he has overcome his final objections, a prospect will make a buying *decision*, either yes or no. Buyers don't close sales. They make buying decisions.

> Great salespeople never try to sell something to someone. That's a push.
>
> Great salespeople think like a prospect and help them make a buying decision.

It really is that simple. You go along with the process and pull a prospect through his buying decision. You help him get to where he wants to go. But you need to pull, not push. You walk him through his buying process; you do not sell him anything.

Now it's time to put some tools in your tool kit.

The Process^{Tool}
VEA Worksheet

Initiate: _____

_____

_____

Educate: _____

_____

_____

Justify: _____

_____

_____

Validate: _____

_____

_____

Close: _____

_____

_____

The Process^{Tool}
TakeAways

1. What did you learn from this tool?

   _____

   _____

   _____

2. What prospect will you use this tool with? In what way?

   _____

   _____

   _____

3. Which people or partners will you share this tool with?
   What will you tell them?

   _____

   _____

   _____

4. What will you change based on using this tool?

   _____

   _____

   _____

The Beginning

"Sales are won or lost early in the sale."

"I can tell if the prospect is with me or not after the first few minutes of a sale."

"Those first few minutes are critical. If I can't create an interest with the prospect after the first few minutes, it's all downhill from there."

You know that the first part of any sale is the most important. You practice your opening pitches, your question-asking techniques, and your rapport-building skills so those crucial first few moments of a sale go well. Well, here's some bad news: Those first few moments go well for about 20 percent of you. For the rest of you, it's often a matter of

* Show up and throw up

* Spray and pray

- Shotgun and hope

- MindMeld ("If I could just get everything from my head into your head, you'd know why you should buy from me.") Just like Mr. Spock in Star Trek.

For all of you, it's time to look at the beginning of a sales call, open it up a bit, add some tools to your tool kit, and then practice, practice, and execute.

There are six tools for the beginning of *The Ultimate Sales Tool Kit:*

- BuyThink^{Tool}

- PowerHour^{Tool}

- 30-Second Intro^{Tool}

- 20-Second Intro^{Tool}

- 3 Languages^{Tool}

- RePhrase+^{Tool}

Adding these tools to your tool kit will be easy. Putting them into practice may be a bit harder, since trying something new is often uncomfortable. BuyThink and PowerHour are tools you can put into practice immediately. They are tools for your planning time; your time to get better organized and better prepared. The rest of the tools are execution tools for use during a sales call. They have been designed to get you and keep you in control of a sales call (since most sales calls are really battles for control).

So let's go to the beginning part of a sale, the battle for control. Here are six tools that will make you better.

C H A P T E R

BuyThink^{Tool}

Tool Kit

BuyThink^{Tool}**:** Think like a buyer and get buyers involved in their buying process.

How would you want to be sold to? • What information must you have in order to make a decision? • How do you picture an ideal salesperson selling to you? • Can you think like a buyer and be better prepared to launch a sales call?

Great initial sales calls happen when you tailor your presentation to the buyer—to how he wants to receive information rather than how you want to deliver it. Prospects want to feel they are in control. Heck, it's their money and their decision.

But there's a problem: You want to be in control, too. After all, it's your product or service, and you know exactly how the prospect should use what you are offering most effectively. Watch out: Here comes death by PowerPoint. You certainly have the right answers, the right solution, and the correct fit. Unfortunately, the very "push" enthusiasm that gets you talking gets you in trouble. It has you thinking like, well, a salesperson. It's time for BuyThink.

	THE BuyThink DIFFERENCE	
Trait	**How a Salesperson Thinks**	**How a Buyer Thinks**
Attitude	Enthusiastic	Probing
Direction	Pushing information	Pulling information
Focus	All about the product/service	All about themselves
Timing	Short term	Long term
Goal	Solution provider	Solution solver
Orientation	Feature/benefit	Mutual benefit
Results driven	Commission based	ROI based
Objective	Value provider	Value maker
Next step	Contract signed	Agreement reached

Okay, you get it. But what specific, tactical things can you do to execute this tool effectively? There are three "how to" things you can specifically do to get into the BuyThink mode.

* IQs

* DOs

* GAS

PREPARE TWO IMMEDIATE QUESTIONS (IQs)

What's on a Prospect's Mind Right Now?

No, this is not two IQ questions about you, your product or service, or why the prospect should take your call. Nor is it about "what keeps them awake at night," but that's closer than you think. You have to be the buyer. What is she thinking about? What worries her? What are her goals right now? Why does she get up in the morning and go to work? What does she think about as she drives to work every morning?

Sit at her desk and think what her #1 priority is?

...Or even better: What's her boss's No. 1 priority?

IQs are the questions that are important to buyers right now. They are working on a solution to something right now, and they are missing some pieces. Imagine a jigsaw puzzle that's supposed to have 500 pieces, but came with only 481 in the box. Buyers need to know where to find the missing pieces since they do not want to throw away the entire puzzle. They've worked too hard on it to throw it all away and start over. That's what most "push" salespeople assume buyers will do when they hear how great their product or service is.

This is called a Solution Box. The prospect's version and your version are different. You believe the prospect has a NEED, and if you can solve 90+ percent or more of the need, you'll get the order.

Well, prospects don't think like that. Prospects already have 80+ percent of their jigsaw puzzle complete. If you can just supply them with one or two of the missing pieces, everybody wins.

What are they working on? What pieces of the Solution Box are they missing? Don't ask what are their pain points or their hot buttons; prospects don't think like that. Prospects never ask themselves, "What are my hot buttons?" Be real.

Ask them what help they need with their puzzle, and they'll tell you. They need to find the missing pieces. Do a little homework and prompt them with information about what other customers are working on and they will open up even more.

Some IQs are:

- What is on your desk today/this week?

- What is critical to your boss today/this week?

- What meetings are taking up most of your time nowadays? (If they are spending time, it's important.)

- What are you telling others who can help you to do today/this week? (This can be peers, friends, employees, or relatives for that matter.)

- What are you working on that is a priority right now?

- What are you working on that needs to get implemented?

Keep the scope of your questions limited to these areas and you'll have your prospect talking about problems that need to be solved, not just things that need to be provided or purchased.

"Solved" implies a mutual win-win, a pull. "Provided" suggests dumping something in their laps, sending them a bill, wishing them luck, and charging them for service even if they can't figure out what they got. That being said, prospects know you're getting something out of the sale too. You are pulling together. Don't go overboard, but everyone knows you are providing a mutual benefit—and that's okay.

DECISION OPTIONS (DOs)

What Decision Options Does the Prospect Have?

What if you were chartered to come up with some options for your prospect, only one of which could be your solution? We are not talking about proposing a solution that is in direct competition with you, since you will fight that battle on a feature/benefit playing field. (Which is where your marketing department wants you to fight, but your prospect never does.)

What are some decisions the prospect can make, and what would be the outcomes? Imagine he called you in for a consultation and gave you an assignment to come up with three recommendations. He'll pay you a commission if he buys your solution, but he'll pay you three times your commission if you come up with three recommendations from which he can choose. Only one of the DOs has your solution, and all three have to be really good. What noncompetitive options would you recommend? What decisions would you and they make, and how would you both get to a decision point?

Your prospects always want options, or choices. Working with them, you will be seen more as a partner than a pushy salesperson. Just ask them: "What are some of the more feasible options you are looking at to address this problem?" That will get them talking.

GREAT ACTION STEPS (GAS)

Now That a Decision Has Been Made, How Would a Prospect "Step on the GAS?"

What would they do first? How would they use what they are looking to buy? What would they do second and third? By knowing your buyers' GAS, you are really thinking like they are thinking.

Again, this is not, "How are they going to implement what I am selling them?"

"How are they going to implement what I am selling them?"

This is, "Okay, I found some more pieces of the puzzle. What do I do with them? How do I use these new pieces? How do I get started in small incremental steps?"

Thinking about GAS will get you in the buyer's car, heading in the buyer's direction, with you taking the lead about where to go first, second, third, and all the way home. Be a piece in their puzzle; they will value that. Try to be the whole puzzle, and well, that's not really what they are working on right now, so don't plan on getting their attention, their time, or the sale.

THE CAMERA

Sam needed to buy a new camera. His kids were playing sports, and the camera he had did not take multiple consecutive pictures well. It was too slow, and when in multiple picture mode, the camera screen went black, so he could not see what he was taking multiple pictures of. Bottom line: gotta have all those special moments on film.

Salesperson #1 was an expert in photographic equipment. He told Sam all about the lenses, the cameras, the brand differences, the feature differences, and the price differences. ASO, F-Stop, light meters—there was a lot to learn. This salesperson was very educational, really knowledgeable, very helpful, but did not get the sale.

Salesperson #2 was all about price. She assumed Sam knew what he wanted. Heck, he said he did; so she went right for the sale and offered "the best price." She even knew how to get Sam to agree she offered the best deal. And though it was the lowest price and a great package, the sale escaped her as well.

Obviously, salesperson #3 made the sale. He asked Sam why he needed a $1,000 camera. What was he going to use it for? He asked IQs and found out that football season and volleyball season were underway, and that Sam was unhappy with the pictures he was taking.

The salesperson also learned from Sam that pictures he took during volleyball, which was played indoors with no natural light, were turning out too "yellow" with his old camera. Also, he didn't get a lot of "great moments" during the volleyball games or on the football field. He also found out Sam's friend had gotten a new camera and was very pleased with the new results.

The salesperson gave Sam a decision option and told him he had two options. One was to keep what he had and learn to use the camera better. There would still be limitations, but it would get better. There were some books he could read, or some classes he could take. Next, he discussed a new camera option with Sam, and talked with him about how it would solve almost all of his picture-taking problems.

Then, he stepped on the GAS. He told Sam what to do first if he took the camera home. He told him to play around with it, get comfortable with it. To explore all the options, but find three that he really liked, then come back to the camera store in a week and they would together decide if the value Sam was looking for was being met. Sam went home that night knowing he had a partner. He had found someone who was thinking about him, pulling with him, rather than someone just pushing cameras.

BuyThink^{Tool} is more than just what to do, it is a concept through which you can take positive, proactive steps toward becoming more successful at the start of a sale.

BuyThink^{Tool}
VEA Solution Box

Your View of the Solution You Think the Prospect Wants

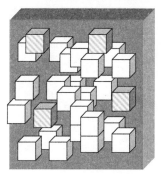

Solution Value to Prospect = $1.0m

Your Prospect's View of His Own Needs.

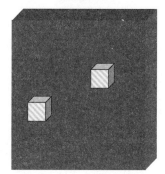

Solution Value to Prospect = $30m

The prospect's IQs:

_____

_____

The prospect's DOs:

_____

_____

Step on the GAS by:

_____

_____

BuyThink^{Tool}
TakeAways

1. What did you learn from this tool?

_____

_____

_____

2. What prospect will you use this tool with? In what way?

_____

_____

_____

3. Which people or partners will you share this tool with?
   What will you tell them?

_____

_____

_____

4. What will you change based on using this tool?

_____

_____

_____

PowerHour^{Tool}

Tool Kit

PowerHour^{Tool}: **Successful time management tool in one hour a day.**

How do I find great prospects? • When can I call them? • When should I focus my best efforts? • How do I make sure I spend the right amount of time on the right prospects? • Where do I get a few more hours in a day?

It's 8:00 a.m., time to start the day. What's the first thing you do?

- Review e-mail

- Listen to voice-mail

- Return calls to prospects who called you yesterday

It's now 10:45 a.m. and you have accomplished only what others want from you. You are marching to someone else's drum. You have not done anything proactive, and you wonder why you are not ahead of the game. Welcome to PowerHour.

Time management is a discipline. You know you need to get better at it, but you never find the time. Why? You go back to your old safe routine, your success patterns. You resort to actions and strategies that reaped success. You go back to the reactive addiction. You feel good reacting to others, since that is a behavior that made you successful. You feel a sense of accomplishment completing a task someone has given you. Well, no more.

WHALES

PowerHour is where you spend one hour a day, five hours per week doing something for you, focusing on your top deals and your top prospects. In Las Vegas they're known as "whales," since they are very big spenders or have the potential to spend a lot of money. There are whales out there you know you should spend some time on, and if you did spend some time on them, you know you would land one. You just don't have the time...blah, blah, blah. You need to do something—anything—to move these prospects along. THESE ARE YOUR BEST. Do something about them!

Sometimes it seems overwhelming to move these major deals along, so PowerHour is a natural opportunity for you to spend some quality time with these prospects.

Isn't it amazing how most companies come up with their major accounts programs?

> "Okay, so who are our biggest accounts? Who is doing a
> lot of business with us? Gee, if they are spending that
> much with us already, they must have the ability to do
> more."—**Reactive**
>
> "Okay, what accounts are out there that we want—and that
> our competition may have as well?"—**Proactive**

Go after not only the current prospects you are working on
but the ones you really want on your customer list—your own
major accounts, your whales.

The secret to making PowerHour work effectively is to
change your physical environment. Your current environment is
reactive; you are set up to respond. During PowerHour, go to a
coffee shop or a conference room, anywhere but your office. The
change to a new environment may seem awkward and a bit
strange, but you will be at your best because of it.

TRUE STORY

"To me, success meant being so busy I had a list of things to do
a mile long. When I began each day, I hit the ground running.
There was no time to be proactive. I felt like a hamster in a
treadmill. The faster I went, the more productive I felt. But really,
how much faster could I go?

"I knew then I had to try something different, so I decided
to change some things. I work out of my home and had become
a creature of habit: Get up, make coffee, go into the office, look
at e-mail, listen to voice-mail, organize my day, and then get on
the most important issues facing me. It was a very effective way
of doing things, and it worked for me. The problem was my
pipeline had begun to dry up, so I was filling it with medium to
small deals and telling myself it would be cleared up soon,
and that then it would be back to smooth sailing.

"Silly me.

"The way I really got proactive and got out of my slump was to have coffee every morning outside the office. There is this small coffee shop around the corner that is not too busy, so I go in there every morning at 7:30 a.m., sit in the corner, have a coffee, and focus either on my important deals or the companies I really want to get into. I usually get to do this three to four times per week, and since I put the coffee machine away at home, if I really want coffee in the morning (and I do), I have to go to the coffee shop. And when I go there, I have to have a PowerHour. I am now into a routine where if I don't have a PowerHour in a few days, I feel weird—and I miss my coffee. Being proactive, using PowerHour and changing my venue, made me change a reactive habit, and it's been very successful. It works."

For every salesperson, there are three major areas of prospects and customers.

1. The most lucrative: big opportunity and big risk.

2. The middle of the pack: repeat customers, medium prospects. The majority of your customers and prospects are here.

3. The area of most activity: low risk, since this is where salespeople are following up, handling problems, setting up things. This is where salespeople tend to spend the majority of their time.

In *ProActive Selling,* I called this most lucrative area the Red Zone, which is where whales swim. In *Knock Your Socks Off Prospecting* we identified hunters (prospecting salespeople) back in the days of the old west. To the Native-American hunter, buffalo was the prized game, therefore in *KYSO Prospecting,* we identify the Buffalo Zone. Now we are calling them Whales, or the Whale Zone, if you like. Actually, it doesn't matter how you label it, as long as you:

1. Designate your really important prospects for the month or quarter and work only on those during this hour.

2. Spend your PowerHour activities focused on whales who spend a lot of money—but not with you. Or focus on current whales who are not doing much with you but have the potential for it.

3. Change your environment. It may feel strange, but the gain will supersede your feeling, especially when you start getting appointments. Change is hard, but once you do it, you'll be asking yourself why it took you so long.

4. Share your results. Other people will share in your success and will imitate it, which makes it even more of a habit. Tell your boss too, to get support and encouragement for the change and success you achieve!

Most salespeople are reactive by nature. They react to the wishes of the company, of their boss, or of their current prospects. By definition then, salespeople are being told what to do and how to do things all the time. If not, you would have two or three whales right now.

Go get your boat, go down to the conference room, the coffee shop, or wherever you need to get away, and spend one hour today doing nothing—nothing but finding whales.

PowerHour^Tool
VEA Worksheet

The account I am focusing on right now.

Whale: _____

Initial Contact Made: _____
❏ ❏ ❏

Homework Level 1: _____
❏ ❏ ❏

Homework Level 2: _____
❏ ❏ ❏

E-Mail Sent: _____
❏ ❏ ❏

E-Mail Sent: _____
❏ ❏ ❏

E-Mail Sent: _____
❏ ❏ ❏

E-Mail Sent: _____
❏ ❏ ❏

Voice-Mail: _____
❏ ❏ ❏

Presentation: _____
❏ ❏ ❏

Presentation: _____
❏ ❏ ❏

Sent Info: _____
❏ ❏ ❏

Special note on using the PowerHour VEA Worksheet: The power of three is well documented, so on the PowerHour VEA Worksheet, you will notice three boxes on each line. Cross off each box each time you accomplish one of the line's goals. Then you can track your own progress.

PowerHour^{Tool}
TakeAways

1. What did you learn from this tool?

_____

_____

_____

2. What prospect will you use this tool with? In what way?

_____

_____

_____

3. Which people or partners will you share this tool with? What will you tell them?

_____

_____

_____

4. What will you change based on using this tool?

_____

_____

_____

30-Second Intro^{Tool}

Tool Kit

30-Second Intro^{Tool}: How to start a sales call.

How do I get a sales call off on the right foot? • How do I get the prospect to believe I can help him? • How do I make sure prospects get interested and start talking with me, showing me, and explaining to me how they want to buy?

It is all about them. It cannot be said enough. It is all about them. If you mention:

I...	I think...
I need...	So, what I would like to do...
I believe...	I have heard...
What I really need to know...	

You have it all wrong. You should cringe every time you mention the word "I." Why?

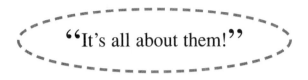

Using the word "I" implies a one-way conversation, and worse, it puts the conversation's focus on you and not the customers; and they want the focus on them...them, them, them, them, and them.

Your No. 1 job is to make the customer feel SIGNIFICANT. That's a big word, but you need to make your customers and your prospects feel significant, and you can't do that by talking about, well, you.

Start each sales call with an introduction that focuses on them, and gets them talking about what's important to them. Follow the three steps of a 30-Second Introduction.

1. Intro

2. 3/3

3. Summarize and Flip

INTRO

Keep Your Introduction Short and Sweet

No need to ramble all about...you.

> "Hi, this is Skip Miller."
>
> "Hello, Mr. Carlyle, I'm Skip Miller."

That should be about it.

3/3

Tell Them Three Things About You, and Then Get Them Involved by Asking Three Questions

Providing three things about you to frame the conversation and to give the prospect an outline of what the conversation is going to be about puts the prospect in the right frame of mind and keeps him from guessing what this sales call is about.

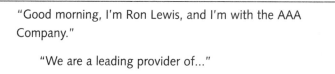

> "Good morning, I'm Ron Lewis, and I'm with the AAA Company."
>
> "We are a leading provider of..."
>
> "We have been in business for...and"
>
> "Our mission is to..."

Again, short and sweet. Time yourself; you should not spend more than 10 seconds here. That's it. Set these anchors and get to the real interesting part of the speech: them.

A quick note on how to get to the 3/3. You are not just going to blurt out your 3/3 right as soon as you meet someone, or the second she picks up the phone.

You want to take a few seconds and set the tone of the call. Use one of the following:

- The permission

- The reference

- The call to action

- The need to help

- The homework

- The expert

There are others to be sure. But these seem to be the most effective, so develop your own style by adapting one or two to use in your tool kit.

After your first "3" introduction, the second part of 3/3 is about creating interest with the prospect. Make her start to think about herself, so she'll feel comfortable about starting up a conversation with you. You make the prospects think and get involved with questions about them. What are they asking themselves about what they need, what they would like, or even what they are doing on a daily basis?

There are two steps to 3/3: first a bridge, then the questions.

1. Bridge. The "/" between 3/3 is what we call a *bridge*. It's the transition between how you are introducing yourself (the first 3) and getting the prospect involved enough to talk (the second 3). A bridge phrase shifts the attention.

"You are probably wondering..."

"A lot of people we talk to have questions such as..."

"Research shows that what's on people's minds right now is..."

"Currently, my customers are asking me questions such as..."

"Executives like you have been asking us..."

Whatever you are comfortable with will come across best to the prospect. A bridge phrase then leads into the questions.

2. Questions. This where you get prospects focused on their favorite topic: THEM!

> "How can I do more with less?"
>
> "Is there a company that can deliver on time?"
>
> "How can I make my current budget go further?"

These are just three basic questions. Yours can be more elaborate and involved. Just make sure your questions focus on what the prospect is thinking about. What is the prospect thinking about on her way to work, during lunch, during all those endless meetings? You have to forget about you and think about what's on the prospect's mind. These questions should never be about you:

> "What can my company do...?"
>
> "How can I help...?"
>
> "What can I do...?"

If the questions are all about you, your prospect may feel that you are a boor. She'll feel left out because all you talk about is, well...you.

Have you ever seen the Gary Larson cartoon of what we say to dogs and what dogs hear? The top panel is the dog owner saying something to the effect, "Ginger, bad dog, musn't eat my slippers. Bad Ginger, bad, bad dog." The bottom panel shows what the dog hears, "Ginger blah blah blah, Ginger blah blah."

That same feeling holds true for the prospect.

With all due respect to G. Larson:

**What we say
to prospects...**

**What they
hear...**

So what I want to do today, and would like to know, and what I would like to cover is our GR 400...

I, I, blah, blah, today I, I, I... I, I know, blah, blah, blah...cover...blah, blah, GR 400...I, I...blah

Sit in the prospect's chair; lean back and imagine you are going to have a meeting with you. What would be on your mind? What questions would you have before you met with you?

"I wonder if they can solve my problem?"

"I wonder if they can save me money?"

"I wonder if they can help me figure out..."

You would never agree to meet with you unless you had a question formulated in your mind. What do you think prospects want to do, listen to you?

No. They want to talk! Let them.

That's what you want to put on the table first, and you do this by paraphrasing questions that are on a prospect's mind. How do you know what's on her mind? Well, you have a ton of experience with these kinds of prospects, since many of them are your customers right now. Go back and ask them why they bought from you. What problems were they trying to solve? What did they do with your product/service? There are your three questions.

Bridge and 3

"Mr. Hamilton, we talk to executives like you a lot, and the questions we hear are:

How can I decrease my cycle times in my current product line?

Is there a way to lower my inventory costs today?

How can I save time on getting my current product to market?

"We hear these questions quite often, but before we get into these, what are some of the things that you need to deal with currently?"

Practice in a mirror and practice on your voice-mail. Listen to yourself! These questions have to be all about the prospect. He has a question on his mind, or he's curious, which is why he is meeting with you, taking your call, or answering your e-mail. He's not interested in you. Ask questions, and then summarize the conversation. Then get him talking by asking the end question, which is called a "Flip."

Your prospects want to hear a 30-Second Intro. They want to know who you are and then they want the floor. Use this tool to let them talk. You stay in control and they feel great. Nice tool!

30-SECOND INTRO

"Good morning, Ms. Fletcher. My name is Skip Miller, and Ron Mills told me to give you a call. I'm with Track Corporation, and at Track, we:

* Offer a complete line of office products

* Have 24-hour shipping

- Offer the most competitive prices in the area

"The reason I am calling you is because we talk to a lot of office managers, and the questions we usually get are:

Is there an office supply company that can get me exactly what I need?

Can they get it to me fast?

Can I make sure I am getting the most up-to-date product and pricing when I order it?

"These are questions we often hear. But before we get into these, what are the issues you have today with your office supplies?"

30-Second Intro^{Tool}

VEA Worksheet

Introduction:

_____

_____

_____

3/:

1. _____

2. _____

3. _____

Bridge: _____

/3:

1. _____

2. _____

3. _____

Summarize and Flip: _____

_____

_____

30-Second Intro^{Tool}
TakeAways

1. What did you learn from this tool?

   _____

   _____

   _____

2. What prospect will you use this tool with? In what way?

   _____

   _____

   _____

3. Which people or partners will you share this tool with?
   What will you tell them?

   _____

   _____

   _____

4. What will you change based on using this tool?

   _____

   _____

   _____

20-Second Intro^{Tool}

Tool Kit

20-Second Intro^{Tool}: **What an effective voice-mail or e-mail should look like to have the best chance of success.**

How do I leave an effective message so they call me back? •
Can I use e-mail to start a sales process? • How can I quickly get
someone's attention when they have little or no time?

Another tool you will need in your
tool kit is a short and powerful
introduction when the prospect
can't be reached directly or you
are really short on time. This
would include voice-mail, e-mail,
an admin screen, letter, fax, bump-
ing into him or her, or any other

communication you might have with the prospect short of an interactive two-way conversation.

The 30-Second Intro is a strong tool to use for a live sales call, but the 20-Second Intro is more compact, more about the prospect (less about you!), and will encourage the prospect to get back to you—or at least to be more receptive to your next contact.

WHY DO YOU NEED A 20-SECOND INTRO?

Because you are always leaving messages about, well, you!

> "Mr. Smith, this is Jim Morris at the ABC Company. What we do is..."
>
> Hey there, Mr. Smith, Judy Dell from Midwest Supply calling you to tell you about our..."
>
> "Hi, Mr. Smith, my name is Syglkb Bghuiwef..." (Go ahead and try to understand people who mumble their names.) Prospects who don't understand your name won't call you back.

Poor cold-calling behavior and poor results are really not your fault. Just look how you have been trained. If you remember, you got inundated with marketing hype, brochures, and a ton of information about the product or service you are selling. You got sold on it. You even think it is pretty good stuff. And heck, it usually is!

Then, armed with knowledge and passion, you make a mistake. You start believing, really believing. You believe that the same tools, the same message, and the same technique that convinced you of your product's greatness will convince your prospect too.

Wrong!

Your prospects have to figure it out for themselves. The reason you got sold on your products and services is because you had questions:

- "What is it that I am selling?"
- "How does it work? How is it used?"
- "What does a customer do with it?"
- "What value does a customer get from it?"
- "What does the competition have, and how are we better?"

Then, with your head full of these questions, you spent quite a bit of time learning what you offer and what it means to your prospects and customers. You learned and took ownership.

The problem with most sales approaches is that they begin with answers, while most prospects—like you in the training class—begin with questions. So, armed with answers, the questions you typically ask are the wrong ones:

"Mr. Smith, you are probably wondering:"

- "What can I do for you?"
- "Why our system works the best?"
- "What specific application you can use our product with?"
- "How you can get maximum value with our product?"
- "Why we are better than the competition?"

Good idea on the questions, but you are starting with a base of knowledge the prospect does not have. They have no idea what you are talking about, nor do they care. They have questions without your answers, so anticipate and ask the kinds of questions that are on their minds right now.

- "What is it that I need right now?"

- "How does it work? How is it used?"

- "What can I do better than I am currently doing?"

- "How can I keep lowering costs and increasing revenue without taking on risk?"

- "What does the competition have, and how are we better?"

Get their attention in a 20-Second Intro by asking questions that will resonate with them, not you.

A 20-SECOND INTRO

The Pattern-Interrupt Version

The pattern-interrupt is designed to ensure a customer's focus.

"Hi Mr. Trah, I'm Skip Miller from the XXX Company. The reason for my call is to answer any questions you may be asking yourself, like:

How can I shorten my lead times on my new product design?

Is there a way that I can increase my revenues in a timely manner?

> *Can I really reduce lead times and lower my overall costs at the same time?*
>
> "If these are questions you are currently facing, please call me back at 555-1212. Thank you for you time."

Quick, to the point, and all about them! That's how to get the prospect to call you back, all in three steps.

Step 1—Quick Intro

Keep it short. Get out of this part of the conversation in less than five seconds.

Step 2—The Questions

"The reason for my call is to answer any questions you may have...

1. _____

   _____

2. _____

   _____

3. _____

   _____

First, the pattern interrupt:

> "The reason for my call" interrupts the prospect's pattern. It's like when you listen to a speech and all of a sudden the speaker says something like:

> "...first..."
>
> "...and in conclusion..."
>
> "...to summarize..."
>
> "...and finally..."

These pattern interrupts get the attention of the listener. Imagine that, like your prospect, you are on the receiving end of a prospecting call.

> "Hello, Mr. Miller, my name is Don Lynch and I'm with XXX. XXX is a company that provides blah, blah blah..."

This is a typical sales prospecting speech. However, with a pattern interrupt, the attention of the prospect gets refocused.

> "Hello, Mr. Miller, my name is Don Lynch and I'm with XXX. The reason for my call is to answer questions you may have regarding..."

Now the focus is on the prospect's questions. And since they are the prospect's questions, well heck, the prospect may even listen. He won't listen to statements about you, so with a pattern interrupt and questions (which he has) about him (his favorite topic), you stand a much better chance of a return call. Use whatever you feel comfortable with; just avoid the word "I."

Typical pattern interrupts that can be used here include:

"The reason for my call/e-mail..."

"The purpose of my call to you..."

"The intent of this e-mail..."

"The objective of this e-mail..."

"The goal of this call..."

The second part of Step 2 is about questions rather than statements. Just like in the 30-Second Intro, questions go to a part of the brain that makes a person wonder, "Am I asking myself these questions?" That's what you want your prospect to think. By asking questions, you are already starting to transfer ownership, since you are asking her if she herself asks these same questions.

Again, do NOT use statements here. Statements go to a yes/no binary part of the brain. ("Yes, I agree with that statement," or "No, I do not agree.") That won't encourage the prospect to think, take ownership, or be inquisitive. Statements are patterns that prospects are used to, and they will more than likely cause them to take no action.

Step 3—Call to Action

Short, sweet, to the point, effective, and all about them. Do NOT say, "So what I would like to do..." Please, no "I's"; keep the focus on them. Use the words "we" or "you"; never "I" or "my." "I" and "my" are words that imply you are either sending or listening to one-way communication. And that's not what you want here. When you say, "What I want..." you are not including the other party. As a matter of fact, you are demanding, which may turn prospects off. Stick with "you" and "we," and you'll get more conversations.

After a day or so, this will become very natural. It's like riding a bike. You know you need to, and once you get it you'll ask yourself why you waited so long.

A 20-SECOND INTRO

The Help Version

Another way to approach a 20-Second Intro is to ask for help. People, prospects, even our mothers want to help us. It's people's good nature to try to help others. Your prospects will help you. All you need to do is ask.

The structure of a 20-Second Help Intro is pretty straight-forward.

> "Mr. Trah, my name is Skip Miller. I am an executive account manager from XXX Company and I could use your help.
>
> "I've been talking to some people in your company, and some questions have come up regarding your:
>
> 1. Go-to-market strategy
>
> 2. Current sales model
>
> "I can be reached at XXX–555-1212. Please call me back at your earliest convenience."

Step 1—Intro

The beginning part should be your quick introduction and your call for help.

> "Mr. Trah, my name is Skip Miller. I am an executive account manager from XXX Company and I could use your help.
> I've been talking to some people in your company..."

If you want to use some other help statements, try these:

> "I've been doing some research on your company."

> "I've got some questions regarding..."

"John Smith in your marketing department and I have been talking, and some questions came up..."

Use whatever help statements you feel comfortable with.

Step 2—Help Type

Now is the time to describe, briefly, the help you need.

"...and some questions came up regarding your:

1. Go to market strategy

2. Current sales model

Use whatever help-type statements or questions you believe are applicable and will generate a callback. They should apply to the tasks and duties at which the person you are calling can be helpful. Of course, there's no need to ask prospects for help in areas where they can help you but have no relevance to your product or service. It would be kind of stupid, as well as dishonest, to call a VP of Marketing, asking for help, when your product or service is only useful to a factory worker on the shop floor. Have integrity when you are asking for the type of help you need.

Step 3—Call to Action

This is a simple call to action:

"I can be reached at XXX–555-1212. Please call me back at your earliest convenience."

Keep it short, simple, and to the point. You have used up most of your 20 seconds getting them interested in calling you back. No need to go on talking about you!

A REPRESENTATIVE FROM A MAJOR CORPORATION

Using the 20-Second Intro help version is great. It's unbelievably effective at getting the prospect to call you back. I like when I ask for help. The messages I leave are a request for help, and I get about 80 percent of the people I call to call me back. The psychology is that MOST human beings want to help. It's proactive and not an infomercial. As you know, if you leave an infomercial, the prospect has two choices: either call you back or hit the delete command, and I already know which option they'll choose.—**Joe Moulton**

Both versions of the 20-Second Intro are tools in your tool kit for you to master. Just like any new set of tools, each has its unique strengths and purpose.

The main goal of the Pattern Interrupt 20-Second Intro is to have the prospect take your second call. The research is overwhelming that prospects want the salesperson to keep trying to get in touch with them. The Big Myth of prospecting is the salesperson's belief that the prospect does not want to hear from her. Sorry to burst that bubble, but the research does show that when left a good 20-Second Intro, a prospect is tremendously more receptive to the salesperson's second and third attempts. And if the prospect calls you back, well hey, that's a side benefit!

In some cases, the goal of the Help version is for the prospect to call you back. I guarantee you will dramatically increase the number of callbacks you get with the Help version. The danger of using the Help version is that if a prospect calls you back and gets your voice-mail, the momentum you generated with your call for help sinks rapidly. To use the Help version of the 20-Second Intro effectively, you need to make sure you are in a position to take the prospect's callback. If you are in meetings a lot, or it is generally hard to reach you, you may want to stick to the Pattern Interrupt version.

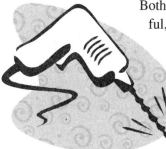

Both 20-Second Intros are very powerful, and they work. Use the tool. Take some time to get familiar with both versions, and then use the right tool for the right job.

The 20-Second Intro tool is like a power drill. There are still people drilling holes with manual drills. Some folks still assemble Christmas or holiday toys with old-fashioned screwdrivers and wrenches. But once mastered, that power drill/screwdriver becomes a go-to tool. So does the 20-Second Intro. Use it and watch your success grow and your productivity radically increase.

20-Second Intro^{Tool}
VEA Pattern Interrupt Version

Introduction:

_____

_____

Pattern Interrupt:

"The purpose for my call is to answer any questions you
may have regarding...

1. _____

2. _____

3. _____

Call to Action:

_____

_____

_____

20-Second Intro^{Tool}
VEA Help Version

Introduction:

"Mr. XXXX, I'm _____ and could use your help..."

_____

_____

_____

Help:

"I've been looking at your company, and there are a few questions I hope you can answer."

Your Help Statement/Questions:

1. _____

2. _____

3. _____

Call to Action:

_____

_____

_____

20-Second Intro^{Tool}
TakeAways

1. What did you learn from this tool?

    _____

    _____

    _____

2. What prospect will you use this tool with? In what way?

    _____

    _____

    _____

3. Which people or partners will you share this tool with?
    What will you tell them?

    _____

    _____

    _____

4. What will you change based on using this tool?

    _____

    _____

    _____

3-Languages^{Tool}

Tool Kit

3-Languages^{Tool}: **How to speak the right language on every sales call and appeal to everyone's interest.**

When I am making a sales call, it's as though everyone I talk to speaks a different language. • How do I know the right language to speak to the right person? • When I am calling at the executive level, what do I say?

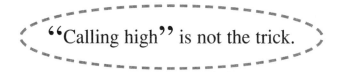

"Calling high" is not the trick.

Anybody can call high. The trick, when you're calling high, is knowing what to say. What do you say to create value and not be sent down to the lower levels of the organization?

57

Salespeople believe if they practice and practice their sales presentation and get more experienced at it, they'll get better and better and make more sales.

That's nice to believe, but customers are smarter than that. Actually, success in sales depends on what customer you are talking to and the language in which the customer is fluent. Customers speak different languages—three, actually. The language a customer speaks depends on what type of customer he is and where he sits in the company's pecking order.

It doesn't matter whether you're selling to an individual, a mom-and-pop shop, a medium-size company, or a large corporation. Of course, things will vary depending on the size of the order and how many people are involved in the decision and other factors, but as a general rule, people you are calling on speak either of (1) features and functions, (2) revenue and costs, or (3) market share and size.

Third Level

Second Level

First Level
(Feature/Function)

THE FIRST LEVEL OF LANGUAGE

The first level includes the people you call on day-to-day. They are the ones who really want to know more about what you do. Typically, first-line managers will be using your product or service, or they will be in charge of its use. They believe they have the most at stake if what you are offering works—or if it doesn't work. Because they have so much at stake, they want to talk about:

* Features and benefits

* Size, shape, color, and weight

- How you compare to the competition

- Quality

- Service and support

- Delivery

- Ease of use

Their necks are on the line, so they're going to want to know everything about who you are and what you are offering. Because you understand this perspective, you, your boss, your marketing teams—pretty much everyone in your company aims their sales and marketing efforts at this level. It's an important level, and, quite frankly, most salespeople are well armed to do battle at this level. Heck, the prospect wants to talk about you; and you want to talk about you. It's a match made in heaven. Most salespeople love making calls at the first level, since it's all about the salesperson, the selling company, and the selling company's products and services.

THE SECOND LEVEL OF LANGUAGE

The second-level language, however, is where conversations always revolve around money. That's all this level cares about: money.

> SALESPERSON: We sell a product/service, they pay us the money, and it's all even. We get the money, they get the product/service, and everyone is happy.
>
> SECOND-LEVEL DECISION MAKER: We give them the money and we get the product/service. What's really important to us is getting our money back. It's why we are buying it in the first place. We need two-to-three times our money back so we can take the profit from this investment and invest in something else so we can make even more money.

Features and benefits? That 44-slide PowerPoint presentation? That really good brochure you just got from Marketing? That demo, free sample, free trial? Not at this level. At this level, it's all about making money.

Money shows up in many different ways. In Chapter 9, ValueStar^{Tool}, we'll cover them.

Third Level
(Market Share/Size)

Second Level

First Level

THE THIRD LEVEL OF LANGUAGE

Third-level people are at the top of the organizational chart. These senior managers ensure the business's stability and growth. They care about market size—how big the market they're going after is; and about market share—how much of the pie they have, how much they want, and how much they can get. That's about it. If they are in a growing market and continue to increase market share (grow faster than the market, that is), they will be seen as visionaries. Their job is to steer the ship into the biggest pond, make sure there are no other big ships around, stake out a territory, and grow an empire. That's why they are captains!

To sum it up, the table looks like this:

Level	Concerns	Questions
First Level	Features/Functions	Can it do this/that?
		How can I get it to...?
		If I have a question, who can I call...?
Second Level	Revenue/Costs	How much time will this save...?
		What are the risks...?
		What is the expected return on this...?
Third Level	Market Share/Size	Will this, in our current market...?
		Can this help us gain share points...?
		How can this, in our new markets...?

Now to keep it simple, it is helpful to label these languages:

* First Level—Let's call it Spanish

* Second Level—Russian

* Third Level—Greek

Okay, who has been on that sales call? Yes, *that* sales call, the one where three Spaniards and you are waiting for a Russian. The

Spaniards are telling you what you need to say and which points to emphasize—all the things they believe the Russian wants to hear. The Russian walks in, nods his head, and signals you that he is ready. With sweaty palms, a bit of a dry mouth, and the fate of the sale resting right on your shoulders, you begin.

"Buenos días, Señor Russian. ¿Cómo está usted?"

You're on a roll! The Spaniards are eating this up. They understand you. They could even give the presentation. Things are going great!

About three minutes into the presentation, the Russian has had enough. This meeting is in Spanish. Why should he waste his time? He gets out as fast as he can.

If you are going to have a meeting and the Russians and/or the Greeks will be in attendance, you'd better make sure that Spanish is not the dominant language.

QUICK MULTILINGUAL HINTS

1. There are some Spaniards who have a Spanish-to-Russian dictionary. They are of great value to Russians, since by having translators around, the Russians don't have to go back and remember how to speak Spanish. You want to involve these "dictionary holders" in your sale.

2. If the Spaniard does not have a dictionary, teach her Russian. If she is unwilling to learn, or if she claims it's not important, you may have to go over her head.

3. Russians are always trying to learn Greek. They want to be promoted, so they want to appear as though they can speak the boss's language.

4. Greeks love to speak Russian, and sometimes even Spanish (mostly Russian though). It lets them feel that they are still involved with the business. Considering that, Russian is the language you should master.

5. Russians want to be called on as early as possible. They are investing people, time, and resources in this purchasing decision. They want to know as early as possible if they are investing wisely. When you talk with them, make sure you ask them questions. And make sure you ask in Russian!

Speak the right language to the right person. When meeting with multiple people, always speak the most important person's language. They are the most important person for a reason.

How do you acquire the ability to speak both Russian and Greek? There are numerous ways.

1. Hang out with Russians—Just hang out and listen. Don't try to join the conversation or you'll be pegged. Just hang out where Russians hang out and listen.

2. Call only Russians during PowerHour—It'll get you away from rationalizing why you aren't calling Russians to begin with.

3. Read what Russians read—*The Wall Street Journal, The Economist,* market share and market size information. Annual reports, quarterly market announcements, even pre-announcements are great sources of Russian and Greek.

4. Informational Interviews—This is a killer idea. Ask some Russians you know—current customers, maybe— for some time. Ask them Russian and Greek questions, and then just listen. (Note: During this interview you

may spot an opportunity for a sale, say, if the Russian inquires about your product or service. This is not a good time to start selling. The Russian will see what you're doing and clam up. If the Russian presents you with an opportunity, try to delay until the end of the meeting, or set up another meeting. There will be plenty of time to provide that missing piece of the Russian's puzzle.)

5. Invite Russians to meet other Russians—Hold a lunch or go to a conference that Russians are attending. Russians love meeting other Russians.

6. Leverage a partner's Russians—Go on joint sales calls with your partners, if you have them. Worst case, meet your partner's Russians. After that, they will know you; they'll see you as someone they can trust.

Learning to speak all languages is important. Fill out the VEA on the three languages during your next PowerHour so you can be fully prepared to speak in your prospect's native tongue.

3-Languages^{Tool}
VEA Worksheet

Greek

Russian

Spanish

What question would you ask each type of prospect?

Spanish Questions:

_____

_____

_____

Russian Questions:

_____

_____

_____

Greek Questions:

_____

_____

_____

3-Languages^{Tool}
TakeAways

1. What did you learn from this tool?

   _____

   _____

   _____

2. What prospect will you use this tool with? In what way?

   _____

   _____

   _____

3. Which people or partners will you share this tool with?
   What will you tell them?

   _____

   _____

   _____

4. What will you change based on using this tool?

   _____

   _____

   _____

RePhrase+^{Tool}

Tool Kit

RePhrase+^{Tool}: Buyers want to make sure they are heard and understood.

How do I make sure the prospect is really in agreement with what I am saying? • How can I get the customer to say those magical words, "Yes, that's exactly what I need!"?

Prospects want to be understood. They want to make sure they are not alone in the world. They need other people to agree with them. They need to have their opinions confirmed, that they have made the right choice. This is never truer than in buying and selling.

Prospects want to make sure the seller meets all of their spoken and nonspoken needs. A prospect says:

Spoken Need	What They Really Mean
"I need it to work 100% of the time."	"If it breaks, how can I make sure you can fix it?"
"I want your best price."	"I'll pay you what you want, just help me get maximum value for it."
"I need it yesterday."	"I'm under a tight time frame. Let me share it with you, and please help."

What prospects say and how salespeople react to these spoken needs is a problem that salespeople face daily. How can they be sure they are interpreting what the buyer says and what he really means? The answer, of course, is to make sure you do not answer the prospect's questions.

"Make sure you do not answer the prospect's questions."

Pretty easy, right?

This is a problem for salespeople. They want to please; they want to help. They believe if they help and please often, they will be selected. Hey, no problem with helping and pleasing. Just make sure you address what the prospect asks of you. Do that and you'll get an order.

RePhrase+ is a communication tool you can use in person, on the phone, in e-mails, and in voice-mails. It is one of the easiest tools to master, and just like a good hammer or screwdriver, it is one you will use quite often. It is divided into two parts: "RePhrase" and "+."

PART 1

RePhrase

The rephrasiing part is simple. You just take what the prospect has told you and rephrase it into a question so she can make sure you heard what she said—and so you can make sure what she actually meant.

Spoken Need	The Need Rephrased
"I need it to work 100% of the time."	"So you are saying you need it to work 100% of the time?"
"I want your best price."	"I hear you. You are saying you want the best price. Correct?
"I need it yesterday."	"Let's review; you are saying you need it yesterday, right?"

By using RePhrase, the prospect will feel she has been heard. When using RePhrase, you must be certain to use the words the prospect uses. No substitutions! If you substitute your words for your prospect's, all you are doing is asking her to interpret something that is not what she said. In that case you have solid grounds for miscommunication, with the prospect feeling like she wasn't heard.

Spoken Need	Sales Interpretation
"I need it to work 100% of the time."	"So you are saying you don't want it to break?"
"I want your best price."	"I hear you. You are saying you want a competitive price, right?"
"I need it yesterday."	"Let's review; you are saying you need it really fast?"

In each one of the examples above, the salesperson's words are different from the prospect's words. Even though the meaning may be the same, the prospect's words have been interpreted, not rephrased. The prospect knows this is not what he said. This opens the door for one of three actions available to the prospect. He will either:

1. Agree, but feel like he has eaten a lemon

2. Argue, and feel that you are not hearing him

3. Get angry, feel frustrated, and go find someone else who understands what he is saying

Salespeople want their prospects to know that they "get it." But when salespeople forget exactly what their prospects say—and then say what the prospects' words meant to them—they risk saying things that the prospects did not mean. It may be a matter of words, but now the prospects have to compare what they said to what the salesperson said. That can be confusing!

Effective sales listening is more than just hearing what the prospect says.

"Effective listening is taking responsibility for knowing what the other person actually meant."

It is all about *them,* and it is your job to make sure they feel they have been heard. By repeating back to the buyer as close as you can their exact words in a question form, a rephrase, you will not only develop those listening skills but make prospects feel they have been heard. And that is a competitive advantage.

Interpretation of questions is a natural thing to do, but it doesn't work very well in the sales world. Break it down into two steps: First, rephrase the question so the prospect feels he is understood without having to figure out what you are saying back. Next, ask a second question. That's the "+."

PART 2

The +

The second part of RePhrase+ is the second question, the clarifying question.

Spoken Need	RePhrase+
"I need it to work 100% of the time."	"So you are saying you need it to work 100% of the time? Why is that important·again?"
"I want your best price."	"I hear you. You are saying you want the best price. Correct? Besides a low price, of course, what do you mean by best price? Could you give me a further definition?"
"I need it yesterday."	"Let's review; you are saying you need it yesterday, right? What is your time schedule again, and what is making this so critical?"

When prospects are throwing out key questions, they want to be heard—and then they want to be understood. Acknowledge that they want to be heard, but then go one step more; ask one more question. Get to what is actually causing them to discuss their needs. There is usually more than one thing making something so important, so critical—and by asking another clarifying question, you'll be amazed how much clarifying information you will get.

Prospects do not want to be heard and understood at the same time. That takes two different steps. Go slow and use RePhrase+ in two different steps: first rephrase the question so the prospect feels she has been heard; and then ask your clarifying question to make sure you "get it." It makes both parties feel warm, fuzzy, and understood.

LEFT-FIELD WORDS^{TOOL} AND RESPONSES

Here is a free tool thrown in for you. It requires active listening. Your goal is to get the prospect to talk about his real issues, not just the superficial ones he tells everyone else about.

The Tool

Why do prospects pick certain words rather than others to describe their needs? Sometimes the words they use seem out of place, out of context, or somehow peculiar. These are known as *left-field words* because they come from an unexpected place.

See if you can pick out the left-field words:

"I need it to work 100% of the time."

"I want your best price."

"I need it yesterday."

"100%," "best," and "yesterday" seem to jump out at you. They are crying for you to ask the prospect what she means. Try these and see if you can pick out the left-field words.

> "I'm happy your product can be delivered in the time frame we need, but the closing costs are really a dilemma for me."
>
> "Yes, that is a solution we can use, and what also is important to us is the flexibility it offers."
>
> "This doesn't seem to be the right time for us to make a total commitment for a product like this."

Responses

Typical sales responses to these questions are usually:

> "I'm happy your product can be delivered in the time frame we need, but the closing costs are really a dilemma for me."
> *"Well, let's see what we can do on those closing costs."*
>
> "Yes, that is a solution we can use, and what also is important to us is the flexibility it offers."
> *"Yes, you are right, the flexibility our T-100 offers is the best in the industry."*
>
> "This doesn't seem to be the right time for us to make a total commitment for a product like this."
> *"Well, what would be a good time to do something?"*

Good answers, but that's the problem: They are answers. RePhrase+ works best when you focus on left-field words and use RePhrase+ in question form.

> "I'm happy your product can be delivered in the time frame we need, but the closing costs are really a dilemma for me."
>
> *"What exactly do you mean by closing costs are a* **dilemma** *for you?"*
>
> "Yes, that is a solution we can use, and what also is important to us is the flexibility it offers."
>
> *"That's great. Could you please tell me what the benefit of* **flexibility** *means to you?"*
>
> "This doesn't seem to be the right time for us to make a total commitment for a product like this."
>
> *"Hmm. What do you mean by* **total** *commitment? I'm not sure I understand."*

By picking out the left-field words and using RePhrase, your true understanding of what the prospect is trying to tell you will come leaping out and smack you right in the face! Nothing like the prospect giving you a little tap to remind you...why they want to buy!

The Role Plays—an Example

It's remarkable when salespeople get together for training. They have a good time and learn new tools. Then, during role plays, they are asked to use the tools they learned in class so the repetitive nature and use of the new tools will sink in and they will feel comfortable using the newly acquired tools in the real world.

Left-field words grew out of my experience conducting role plays. It usually happens during a role-play session when we ask a few of the salespeople to be "buyers" and then have each buyer anchor a sales call with a "team" of two or three salespeople.

We'll tell the "buyers" for example, "If the sales team comes anywhere close to asking about budgeted dollars, you should tell them that Judy April is in charge of the budget, and it is up to her to make this monetary decision."

Well, the role play goes on, and the sales team, anxious to use their new tools, is having a great time with the 30-Second Intro or the 3-Languages™, and they totally miss the budget question. Meanwhile, the "buyer," who has been instructed to make sure the sales team gets the name "Judy April" and understands her decision-making authority, often grows frustrated and begins interrupting the salespeople with statements such as:

> "Well, I'll have to let Judy know about this."
>
> "Thanks again, but for this dollar amount I'll have to get permission."
>
> "It's really not my call for this type of solution."

Left-field words are flying all over the place. But the sales team is so focused on practicing their new tools, or selling features and benefits, they miss the left-field words! It seems really easy in this example, but I have seen so many really good salespeople not actively listen for left-field words that I know this is a tool you need to prepare, practice, and look for during every sales call.

REPHRASE +

"I can't believe I remembered the + sign. I was ready to answer the guy's question. He had asked me a question, which I thought was important. It seemed to come out of left field, so I used the RePhrase tool, and he kept talking for a minute or more. Then, there was this pause, and I knew, I just knew I had an answer for him. Then, I remembered that + sign, so I thought I would ask one more question. Lo and behold if he didn't have one more thing on his mind, and I am sure I would have missed it without that + sign. Thanks to RePhrase+, I made the sale. It's a handy tool to have on initial prospecting calls."

RePhrase+^{Tool}
VEA Worksheet

You need to spend time on this exercise to get this tool, so fill in the blanks.

Spoken need by the prospect:

_____

_____

_____

What you would usually say:

_____

_____

_____

RePhrase:

_____

_____

_____

RePhrase+:

_____

_____

_____

RePhrase+^{Tool}

TakeAways

1. What did you learn from this tool?

   _____

   _____

   _____

2. What prospect will you use this tool with? In what way?

   _____

   _____

   _____

3. Which people or partners will you share this tool with?
   What will you tell them?

   _____

   _____

   _____

4. What will you change based on using this tool?

   _____

   _____

   _____

2

The Middle

"Once the prospect gets interested, the tough part is staying in control and keeping the sale going."

"Staying in control of the sale right up to the end is the toughest thing to do."

"I need to create value, transfer of ownership, and shorten the sales process all at the same time."

The middle part of a sales process is definable as the point when you have made it through the prospecting stage and have entered the education stage. Of course, you want to move through the process and get the sale. You want the prospect to be ready to make a yes-or-no decision.

Two things happen in this stage:

1. *Education:* The prospect and you both get educated: you on his needs and what he is looking for; and he on your products and services.

2. *Transfer of Ownership:* This is where prospects really
   get it. They see what your solutions can do for them,
   and they get very excited. Why, they can almost begin
   selling themselves. And as a matter of fact, they do!

Education is up to you. Most companies do a good job getting
their salespeople enough information about the products and services they offer. Salespeople often complain they have too much,
too little, or not the right information. But overall, they usually do
have enough to educate their prospects.

Educating the salesperson about listening skills, business
skills, communication skills, learning how to craft a solution—
these are the areas that need a few tools.

The transfer of ownership—how to get the prospect to take
ownership of your solution and run with it—is an area that is crying out for tools.

Here are five new tools to help you in these areas:

- TimeZones^{Tool}
- Yes, We Can Do That^{Tool}
- ValueStar^{Tool}
- 3 Stages of Value^{Tool}
- Ask/Tell^{Tool}

Since I have been working with sales and sales managers,
two-way prospect education and transfer of ownership have been
the two most requested skill areas. It seems salespeople are good
at getting appointments (some better than others) and giving presentations. Sales education, educating the prospect on the seller's
features and benefits, is usually pretty well understood.

Getting information from the prospect, getting the right information, qualifying, and completing the transfer of ownership,
well, that's a different story. The tools in this section address these
questions. That said, let's get started.

C H A P T E R

TimeZones^{Tool}

Tool Kit

TimeZones^{Tool}: **Buyers purchase to satisfy needs; and time considerations are a critical, deciding element.**

How can I create a sense of urgency with my prospect? • How do I understand what time sensitive issues are really driving this buying decision? • What do I need to know about the prospect's timing?

Why is it you are always running out of time? Why do you always look at your watch, clock, cell phone, or PDA to make sure you have enough time or can make time, or perhaps even save some time? It seems you run your life with respect to time. So do your prospects. And now you can use time to your advantage.

When they are making a business or purchase decision, your prospects use the entire time spectrum—past, present, and future. Usually they use more than one time element in their decision. Your job is to help the prospect to use time to your advantage.

The TimeZones tool recognizes that time has three zones: past, present, and future. Prospects use these zones to justify their purchasing decisions. They rationalize or compartmentalize their needs, place a priority on them, and then go forth and try to make a decision. Their TimeZone priorities fall into three categories. Each one—past, present, and future—will cause a different motive for buying.

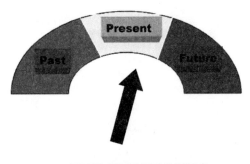

THE TIMEZONES

Past—Decisions made for past motivations are restorative. They are being made to get something back up to speed, to atone for a mistake, to catch up to a standard.

Present—Present decisions are made for present or current reasons. These are ones that take advantage of a current opportunity or a planned scheduled event.

Future—There are a few decisions that are strategic, where prospects will invest now so they can save money or time later, or even defer their risk.

The *restorative, current,* and *strategic* needs of your prospects are all very different. The question is how you can determine what TimeZones are critical to your prospect for making a purchase decision.

The answer is all of them. During a sale, the prospect will give hints and sometimes more than hints that she is looking at multiple TimeZones. It is really quite simple: The more TimeZone issues you face, the more value you create.

> "They said they need it right now because it's holding up production of their new plant."
>
> "He told me, in a very direct way, the reason they are so hot on our solution is they have tried three other options and this is their last attempt. They need to get back on track, and they see us as the way to do that."
>
> "Strategic. I just know it. They are telling me we are critical to the successful launch of the new product they are rolling out in a few months."

Placing your sale in just one TimeZone has limitations. It limits your value. It limits your competitive standing. And it minimizes the justification the prospect is trying to obtain to make a purchase decision. You will have a much better chance of success if you incorporate multiple TimeZones into your presentations, so you can find out the value the prospect is placing in each TimeZone. TimeZone questions that you should ask are:

- Why do you need this right now?

- What has happened that is causing this decision to be made at this time?

- What is currently at the top of the list, and what is causing this to get so much attention?

- Is this the most important need you have that you can see over the next six months?

- Do you see how this will look once we have it installed?

Then listen to the answers! Questions with a time element in them will give you loads of information on where the prospect is in each TimeZone. You need more to your sale than just your product's features and benefits. You need to find out the reason your prospect is willing to make a commitment right now.

Salespeople are always looking for ways to get the prospect moving down a sales path. They are looking to:

- Create a sense of urgency

- Find out the prospect's "hot button"

- Get the prospect back on track

- Find out why the project died

- Figure out why the prospect is not returning their calls

It's easy. You have not asked the right questions to gather up all the value there is from multiple TimeZones. When asked, answers you will probably hear include:

"I need this right away. There are a host of people waiting on me."

"If I can just get some additional memory for the computer, then I don't have to buy a new one."

"This is money well spent. Buying the tickets now, I save 20 percent."

"I don't mind spending a bit more right now, since I know our current plans will use this additional capability in no time."

"With our current budget situation, we have to find a better way."

"Productivity gains must be met. We just have to do more with less."

The answers are present, past, future, future, present, past/present.

There are situations where more than one time consideration must be addressed, and each must be taken care of or the prospect will feel incomplete.

An important note on who sits where on the timeline: It seems the higher you go in the organization, the more future-oriented they will be. A senior manager's job is to live three to six months in the future, and then delegate tasks to junior managers. In Tool Kit language, Russians and Greeks seem to live in the future and present, while Spaniards live in the past and present.

Salespeople are always looking for:

* Hot buttons

* Current pain points

* Hot topics

* Present needs

* Existing concerns

These work well when talking at the first level, but make sure you go to the future when you have an appointment with someone at a higher level. A senior manager wants to know about:

* Strategic needs

* Operational efficiencies

* Planned events

* Future considerations

* Projected actions

These items are way to the right on the TimeZones. If you are going to take the time and effort to talk with a Russian, make sure you have the right timeframe. You can get that by using TimeZones.

Now that you have determined where your prospect sits in relation to time, map it out so you can address the time situation that is most important to her. That visual representation will help you to make sure you satisfy the customer's needs, not just spew what you feel are the most important benefits to her.

TimeZones^{Tool}

VEA Worksheet

Who are you talking to and what is important to them?

Who and What

_____

_____

_____

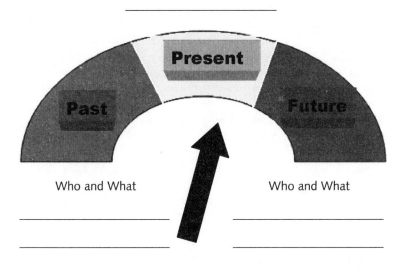

Who and What   Who and What

_____   _____

_____   _____

_____   _____

TimeZones^{Tool}

TakeAways

1. What did you learn from this tool?

_____

_____

_____

2. What prospect will you use this tool with? In what way?

_____

_____

_____

3. Which people or partners will you share this tool with? What will you tell them?

_____

_____

_____

4. What will you change based on using this tool?

_____

_____

_____

C H A P T E R

Yes, We Can Do That^{Tool}

Tool Kit

Yes, We Can Do That^{Tool}: **Prospects want to feel their needs are being met. They want to feel like they are being heard.**

How can I get the buyer to understand that I really get what his needs are? • Is there a way I can be in real rapport with the prospect? • How much value is added by having the prospect believe that I understand his problem the best?

"That's exactly right."

Have you ever heard a more beautiful sentence? When a prospect utters these words, it's like you want to smile from ear to ear. It's like money in the bank, all the tea in China, and winning the lottery all rolled into one.

"So Mary, I heard you say you wanted to:

- Increase your customer service efficiency by 20 percent

- Decrease the 'dropped calls' number by 10 percent

- Get a solution in here that will have that up and running by September 1.

"...Is that right?"
"That exactly right. That's what we have to do...exactly. Is this what you do?"

This is a much better phrase than:

- "Yeah, that's about right."

- "Yeah, kind of."

- "That about covers it."

The list could go on and on. The differences are twofold. First, the first phrase spoken by the prospect has passion. Words and phrases you want to hear from the prospect are:

"Exactly"

"Perfectly"

"Dead right on"

"Precisely"

"Spot on"

The level of interest and excitement the prospect now has leaps out at you, since you have, in her mind, understood fully her problem, her need, and her solution. She is almost relieved that she has found someone else on the planet who thinks the way she does. She has found someone she can share with.

Second, when you come close and the prospect utters words like the following, you have a problem:

"That's close."

"That's a good approximation."

"Uh-huh."

"That's about right."

"Pretty much."

The interpretation is that you are coming close, but you are not really a great fit. So when it gets to decision time, he'll either find someone else or ask for a discount. This is obviously not where you want to be, so here is a tool that can help, in combination with RePhrase+.

"Yes, We Can Do That" is a tool that should be repeated to your prospect just the way it is printed. You use the tool in the requirements phase, or area, of the sale. The prospect is looking for a solution—in fact, he is on a mission—and if someone has the exact answer, just watch his eyes light up.

Think about the earlier example, where you told Mary, in Mary's own words, what she wants to get done and what she is looking for. She exclaims that you got it exactly right. Now is the time to let her feel fulfilled. Not only do you understand her, when she has been trying to be understood for weeks, but you and your company can sell her exactly what she wants. Now is the time when it's okay for a salesperson to give an answer rather than ask more questions. The prospect wants to know that she has been understood.

"Yes, we can do that."

That's all you need to say. That's it. Not how you can do it, why you can do it better than anyone else, or what the details of doing it are.

"THEY DON'T CARE!"

All Mary cares about is that she has found someone who can do it. The match has been made and Mary is—big word here—COMPLETE. Next, she's ready:

1. To move on

2. To be led

Now is the time to connect with the prospect. Be careful to avoid interpretation and droning on and on, which will cause the impact of your "yes, we can do that" to be forgotten.

Interpretation can be good and bad. To take RePhrase+ one step further, if you are going to interpret back to the prospect what his needs are, it's up to you to speak "Buyerese," rather than having the prospect learn to speak "Salesese."

It is good when you can interpret what your prospect has to say and what it means relative to you and your company. If you can figure out what he is saying, and what he really means—and if you can solve it—that's a good thing. That's interpreting Buyerese into your language.

It's bad, however, when you are having a conversation with a prospect, especially when you want him to feel as though you really understand him, and you ask him to translate your Salesese back into his language.

"I want a product that will cover 90 percent of the area I need, come in multiple textures, and be available within 24 hours."

"Okay, so you want this product to cover most of the area, come in both our styles, and be able to get it ASAP. Great, we can do that."

"No, not really. What I want is for it to cover all of this, well, most of it...never mind, you got it, just give me a quote."

Ouch! The salesperson never saw that one coming, and probably will never see that order. You can interpret what the buyer says into your language. In fact, you have to so you can quote back to him what you are going to sell him. However, when you try to get his buy-in before you put that proposal together, you have to keep it in his language if you want him to say:

"That's exactly right."

Droning on and on...this is pretty much self-explanatory.

"I want a product that will cover 90 percent of the area I need, come in multiple textures, and be available within 24 hours."

"Okay, so you want this product to cover most of the area, come in multiple styles, and be able to get it quickly. Great, we can do that. We just developed a new mix that will be just perfect for this application. It just came out a few months ago, and I sold it to another customer a few weeks back, and they tell me that they love it and can't really..."

"That's great...you got it, just give me a quote."

Same deer-in-the-headlights situation in this case too, and don't laugh. Salespeople have this need to help. They believe they have great information that the prospect wants to hear, and when cued up, they just let 'er rip. A good guess is that at least 70 percent of you are guilty of this, so mastering this tool is required.

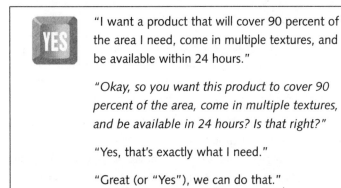

"I want a product that will cover 90 percent of the area I need, come in multiple textures, and be available within 24 hours."

"Okay, so you want this product to cover 90 percent of the area, come in multiple textures, and be available in 24 hours? Is that right?"

"Yes, that's exactly what I need."

"Great (or "Yes"), we can do that."

Deal done. Competitive advantage to you, since the prospect now believes you are offering a solution that perfectly fits her needs because of how you made her feel.

"Yes, we can do that."

Yes, We Can Do That^{Tool}
VEA Worksheet

Xerox this page, and place it on your wall, right by your phone.

Yes, We Can Do That^{Tool}
TakeAways

1. What did you learn from this tool?

_____

_____

_____

2. What prospect will you use this tool with? In what way?

_____

_____

_____

3. Which people or partners will you share this tool with? What will you tell them?

_____

_____

_____

4. What will you change based on using this tool?

_____

_____

_____

ValueStar^{Tool}

Tool Kit

ValueStar^{Tool}: How prospects value and evaluate every solution—in their financial terms.

How can I get the prospect to value what I am selling? • Are how he values a solution and how I present value two different things? • When it really matters, how do senior executives actually evaluate their return on a proposed solution?

Value that the prospect will pay for is the goal that every sales and marketing department seeks. They even call it:

OUR VALUE PROPOSITION

Companies spend millions of dollars, thousands of hours, and countless sales presentations on creating, determining, and substantiating their value. You use reference stories, demonstrations, facts, figures, slides, Excel spreadsheets, and hundreds of other sales and marketing support documents to have the prospect say that the value you are providing is worth your sales price...and then the prospect even acknowledges that he hears you...and then demands a discount.

> **"**Value is not in the eye of the beholder, but in the eye of the one the beholder is trying to influence.**"**

Go to a party and see what kind of beer, wine, or alcohol the host has purchased. Typically, the purchase was made with the guests' tastes in mind, not the host's.

No amount of pushing is going to make the prospect "see" your value. He already has a pretty good idea of how he measures value. The prospect has had to measure value for quite a while and is pretty good at it.

Instead of pushing, get in tune with how the prospect measures value so you can figure out how you should represent it.

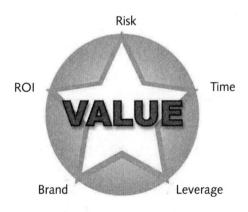

Risk

ROI   Time

Brand   Leverage

Prospects assess value in five ways, and the tool to help you match your products and services to your prospect's definition of value is called ValueStar™.

The ValueStar™ has five points, one for each area in which to question your prospects. This helps define the value your solution provides to them.

ROI—Return on Investment

Businesses judge value by what they get in return for investing their assets. In the business world, ROI is a number. If you invest $100 and get back $120, that's a 20 percent ROI.

In the consumer world, ROI is about numbers and emotions. (If you spend $100 on a friend's wedding gift, you can expect an emotional ROI, not a financial one.)

Since most people already know the value they place on what they're thinking of buying (they're really just looking for valida-tion), you should ask ROI questions. But keep those ROI Excel spreadsheets in your briefcase. You're better off asking questions and getting buyers to tell you what they think the ROI is, since their numbers are the only ones that really count anyway. And Russians and Greeks ALWAYS know the value and ROI before they agree to buy something.

Time

What would you pay for more hours in the day? Prospects will always pay for time. Value-centric salespeople know how their products and services can help their prospects save time. After all, how your offering can affect speed, which is a derivative of time, is of major importance. Truly great salespeople, however, know which time questions will get their prospects talking about their current time issues. Time-related areas of questioning include:

Uptime/Downtime	Time to market
Delivery time	Speed of change
Timing the market	Speed of problem resolution
Catch-up time	Timeliness of a decision
Market upgrade timing	

The list could go on and on. Use time to ask great questions. All managers have time considerations, and they're looking for help. They need some pieces to their Solution Box in regard to time, and they're searching for answers. Just ask them!

Risk

Here's the big one, the one that all prospects want to talk about—and do something about. It is all about risk. Decisions at the lower levels of the organization are very black and white. At the higher levels, they are fraught with risk. This is the number-one issue, by far, with all decision makers.

THE RISK OF REPAIRS

Did you know that car dealers who sell you an extended warranty rarely touch the money you pay them? They bank it, and they earn so much in interest off of what you and other customers pay that when the dealership must cover the cost of a repair, they don't have to touch the principle. The same is true for cameras, computers, software, services, and other appliances with extended warranties. They appeal to your sense of risk. "You just spent $1,000 on that computer," says the retail salesperson. "For an additional $170, we'll cover your risk for another two years." Risk makes money.

Ask prospects about their risks: They'll talk and talk. They are always looking to minimize risk. Decisions would be faster and easier to make if it weren't for risks. Find out what their risks are, address them, and you have a major competitive leg up.

Leverage

If your prospect can find multiple uses for what you're selling, you have just doubled or tripled your value. When printers came out, people loved them and hooked them on to their computers. Then scanners, faxes, and copiers followed. Now, we call them "multi-function devices," since you can get all four for the price of one.

Two is better than one.
2 + 2 = 5
Kill two birds with one stone.

Your prospects have many needs, and some are pretty low on the totem pole. However, if you satisfy a major need and two minor needs, your value has just multiplied. At the very least, you're better than the competition. You've changed how the prospect thinks about what she needs—in your favor.

Brand

What your brand can do for propects is not the question. The value is in what your brand can do to help them implement their strategies and achieve their goals.

You buy a famous brand-name shirt with a logo not just because of its quality but how you will be perceived by others. The same holds true for cars, golf clubs, electronics, art, and the list goes on.

"If I can just have the prospect understand my value proposition..." is not where value lies and should be dropped from your vocabulary.

"If I could just figure out how my product or brand can help them do what they want to do..." is a much better premise! Does your prospect want to be perceived as...

A rebel: Virgin, Apple, UnderArmour

A stable player: Sony, Hewlett Packard, Trane air conditioners, Nordstrom, Home Depot

An up-and-comer: MySpace.com, Tumi Luggage, Tag Heuer

Hip and cool: W Hotels, Google, Mini-Cooper

Kid friendly: Disney, McDonalds

Help your prospect propagate his brand, his message, and you'll create real value.

Value is always up to the prospect. And often what the prospect values and what the salesperson believes the prospect values are two different things. Imagine trying to convince a BMW salesperson that he lost a sale because his cars lack cup holders. He might not be able to imagine that his prospects actually believed that a lack of cup holders makes a car unworthy of consideration! But the fact remains, rational or not, value is always up to the prospect.

Finally, there are two general rules for ValueStar™:

1. *Use questions.* Blurting out the value you can provide is not the same as transferring the value ownership. Your prospects need to figure the value out for themselves. But they need your help, so ask questions.

2. *They know the answers.* Prospects already know the value answers, but there may be features and benefits your prospect doesn't know about. A discussion of

features and benefits can be a good way to educate the prospect about what you do and how you can help.

As we said earlier, value is one consideration that's always defined by the prospect. But prospects often need help in determining how much value there is. They'll have to figure it out for themselves. And once again, asking questions helps. Never tell prospects what your solutions are worth; they have their own ideas of that (and often it's a lot more than what you're charging).

HOW TO USE ValueStar

If you are calling at the right level, your prospect has the points of the ValueStar on her mind all the time.

ROI

What is your current cost of goods sold?

What earning pressures are you under currently?

What processes are costing you the most time and money?

What are your goals for earnings and costs?

Time

What is time sensitive right now?

What issues do you see as time critical?

Where do you see delays causing you the most grief?

How does time impact you the most right now?

Risk

What do you see as your biggest risks in the next few months?

What risks do you face currently with the new products?

What go-to-market risks do you have that seem to elude answers?

How do you know when your risks are the lowest to make a decision on your new designs?

Leverage

How do you evaluate partners currently?

What do you currently have that you feel creates for you the most leverage?

Where do you feel you have the most to gain, but your current processes prevent you from taking advantage of it?

How do you create leverage right now in your current organization?

Brand

How do you derive value from your brand?

What do your customers feel are your competitive advantages and disadvantages?

How do your customers leverage your brand?

What do you see on the competitive horizon that may influence your brand strength?

Other ways besides questions include:

Presentations

A presentation should be loaded with value statements and questions. You should plan time for the prospect to discuss not only his current needs but the value he is losing with these needs not being met, or the value of having the needs met.

"Ms. Davis, what value do you believe your company isn't getting because you do not have this new capability?"

That question will lead to a great discussion and will start Ms. Davis thinking about what value you can provide—not just features and benefits.

Letters, Voice-Mails, and E-Mails

Discussions resulting from value questions should take up 60 to 80 percent of your conversation with a prospect. If you're talking too much about features and benefits, you are allowing the prospect to determine the value of what you have after he gets off the phone or reads your e-mail. Value to the prospect should be discussed early and often!

30-Second Speeches

Value questions with Russians, or revenue-cost decision makers should be the only bottom three questions in a 30-Second Intro. Senior executives think about ValueStar areas all the time, so why shouldn't you ask questions that fall into these areas?

30-Second Intro

Introduction

_____

_____

_____

3/

1. _____

2. _____

3. _____

/3

1. How can I minimize the risks in the marketplace right now?

2. What timing issues does the sales team face this year that could free up 10 percent more revenue?

3. How can I get a better return on my resources than what I am currently getting?

Your /3 questions

1. _____

2. _____

3. _____

ValueStar E-Mail

Dear Mr. Jones,

My name is _____, and I'm with_____.
We are a leader in the _____ industry. We

- Xxx

- Xxx

- Xxx

Recently, many executives have asked us questions such as:

- Is there a way to minimize the risk in these types of decisions?

- How can I get my product to market faster, but maintain the same quality?

- Is there a way I can release the new design, and still maintain the value of our brand?

These are questions we hear quite often, but before we get into these, we would like to discuss further with you some topical issues that may save you time and money while reducing your risk. I will call you in a few days to discuss these and other questions with you.

Regards,

_____

ValueStar^{Tool}
VEA Worksheet

List at least three concerns and issues your prospect has under each topic. This is not about you; it's about what your prospect has a problem with and her or his search for someone or something to solve it.

Risk

_____

_____

_____

ROI   Time

_____   _____

_____   _____

_____   _____

VALUE

Brand   Leverage

_____   _____

_____   _____

_____   _____

ValueStar^{Tool}
TakeAways

1. What did you learn from this tool?

   _____

   _____

   _____

2. What prospect will you use this tool with? In what way?

   _____

   _____

   _____

3. Which people or partners will you share this tool with?
   What will you tell them?

   _____

   _____

   _____

4. What will you change based on using this tool?

   _____

   _____

   _____

3 Stages of Value^{Tool}

Tool Kit

3 Stages of Value^{Tool}: Buyers must quantitatively substantiate value in their own mind, and they need help getting there.

How can I get the prospect to take ownership of the proposed solution? • What are some great questions to help the prospect see the value?

DO YOUR HOW/WHATS

Go ahead. You need to get into shape, so do your How/Whats.

You do pushups, sit-ups, and chin-ups. You do homework, yard work, and house work. You do a lot. You do quite a bit when you are selling. You do proposals, demonstrations, and contracts; sales presentations, cold calls, and closing calls. You do a lot.

""Make sure you do your How/Whats.""

You need the prospect to single you out as the best solution for his need. If he does not see your solution working, the probability of a sale is small. Most companies recognize this and have created presentations and demonstrations to help prospects see how their solution will be of value. You probably do a killer presentation or demonstration to get the prospect to see your solution in the best light, and hopefully recommend your product or service.

Well, there is a tool you can use to accomplish that transfer of ownership in the prospect's mind. Basically, it involves letting prospects use their own minds—getting them to sell themselves. After all, they have a tendency to believe themselves more than they believe you. You proactively induce this transfer of ownership with a questioning technique called How/What.

Salespeople are really good at features and benefits.

> "Our product has this certain feature, and the benefit to you would be..."

This concept is taught in Sales 101 classes all around the world. Make sure you highlight a feature, and then present its benefit. "No one buys a drill, they buy holes" has been a standard cliché for salespeople to remind them to sell benefits, not just present features.

Okay, think about it.

"If you are the one doing all the talking about your features and benefits, then who is taking ownership of the solution?"

You are engaging in one-way communication, acting as though, "If I tell them enough times, they'll get it." Come on.

Your prospect has not taken anywhere near complete ownership in the solution you are providing, or in its value, no matter how many times she nods her head during your presentation. Now is the time to use How/Whats to transfer the ownership and have the prospect develop the value in her own mind. How/Whats go deep to where the prospect really gets it, really gets it and takes ownership.

THE STAGES

To get your prospects to discover the value of your product or service, you have to lead them to it. And remember, they want to be lead to it. They believe they need to discover it themselves, but they really need some help. So, lead them through the three stages of value with your How/Whats.

The three stages of value are how you buy things, so why wouldn't your prospects use the same process when they make decisions?

Prospect's Three Stages of Value

Stage 1—Basic understanding

Stage 2—Taking ownership

Stage 3—Applying value

For the seller, the prospect's three stages involve three parallel stages.

Seller's Three Stages of Value

Stage 1—Agreement

Stage 2—Transfer of Ownership—HOW

Stage 3—Quantifying Value—WHAT

EXAMPLE: THE PROSPECT

The Need: "I need to get a color printer for my home."

Stage 1—Basic Understanding

"I am in agreement with the salesperson that the Canyon QX10 is probably the right one for me."

Stage 2—Taking Ownership

"If I had this at home, HOW would I be working with it?"

- "I could get my work done faster."

- "I could make color copies at home rather than make a trip to the copy store."

- "I could get my work done when I need it done, rather than wait to go to the office."

The Canyon has a good name, and it is on sale. Plus, there's a spot right next to the computer where it would be perfect.

Stage 3—Applying Value

"WHAT would that be worth to me?"

- "Time. I am tired of waiting to go to the office for color prints."

- "I get to keep working when I am focused on getting something done."

- "The kids need to print school work all the time, and our current black and white printer is just not good enough for some of their school projects."

- "I can print color photographs. That's great, because I waste a lot of money and time every year taking my camera to the photo store. That alone is a few hundred dollars."

EXAMPLE: THE SELLER

Stage 1—Agreement

"John, we have just discussed what you are trying to do, and how our QX10 will do what you are trying to do. Would you AGREE?"

Stage 2—Transfer of Ownership—HOW

"HOW do YOU see this working for you? HOW do YOU see your company using this solution?"

Stage 3—Quantified Value—WHAT

"WHAT do you think this is worth to your organization?" "WHAT do you see as the major benefit?" "WHAT do you think this is worth?"

You must go through all three stages—Agreement, Transfer of Ownership, and Quantified Value—if you are to communicate real value, and you must go in the correct order.

"Agreement, How, then What"

The point is not that you watch each specific word you use, but that you go through the Three Stages of Value process. How/What is an easy way to remember to get to the value rather than just a benefit.

3 Stages of Value^{Tool}
VEA Worksheet

Prospect's Three Stages of Value

Stage 1—Basic Understanding:

_____

_____

_____

Stage 2—Taking Ownership:

_____

_____

_____

Stage 3—Applying Value:

_____

_____

_____

3 Stages of Value^{Tool}
VEA Worksheet

Seller's Three Stages of Value

Stage 1—Agreement:

_____

_____

_____

Stage 2—Transfer of Ownership—HOW:

_____

_____

_____

Stage 3—Quantifying Value—WHAT:

_____

_____

_____

3 Stages of Value^{Tool}
TakeAways

1. What did you learn from this tool?

   _____

   _____

   _____

2. What prospect will you use this tool with? In what way?

   _____

   _____

   _____

3. Which people or partners will you share this tool with?
   What will you tell them?

   _____

   _____

   _____

4. What will you change based on using this tool?

   _____

   _____

   _____

Ask/Tell^{Tool}

Tool Kit

Ask/Tell^{Tool}: **Buyers want to be educated and have their decisions validated.**

How can I make sure the prospect is educated? • How can I make sure the prospect really "gets it"? • Is there a way to induce the transfer of ownership proactively?

Prospects treat their Education and Validation as two different steps. In "The Process," we discussed how prospects have a need to educate themselves on a proposed solution and then validate their education process. Ask/Tell will help you with this.

You remember when you had that meeting, right? That really important meeting? The meeting where the prospect seemed to understand exactly what you do, what you are trying to sell, and how your solution will work for him?

- "Yes, I get it. I see what your product does and how we can use it. I get it."

Then you had some more discussion, things got really interesting, and all of a sudden, the prospect cried out,

- "Oh, wait a second, I get it. You mean that if we do this, we can...I get it now."

You know from experience there is a real difference between a prospect who says, "I get it" and one who says:

"I GET IT."

In the first "I get it," the prospect is in the education process. She has a need to understand and figure out what it is you are trying to get her to buy. She's still trying to figure out all the details in what you are offering, too. If the car comes with a GPS system, how does it work? How much coverage does it have? What is the gas mileage? How many cup holders are in the back seats?

Buyers are inquisitive. They get it, but they are still trying to figure it all out. They are trying to get it.

Then, once they get it, they'll need to understand what's in it for them, what they are really going to use it for and how they will need to change to use or implement it. Then, they really "get it."

"Okay, so the car gets 21 miles per gallon and can run on regular gas. Based on my estimated usage, that calculates to under $100 a month, which is perfect."

"Also, the GPS system can be used anywhere in the U.S., so when I go back east this summer, *I can use it for the trip and not have to worry about getting lost, or trying to get the right maps...*"

> *"...and, the screen size of this GPS is bigger than the other one I was looking at, which means I don't have to get out my reading glasses to use it, which means I can..."*

She gets it. This prospect is now in the process of selling herself. Now you use the Ask/Tell tool.

In the car scenario, an overenthusiastic salesperson would take over the sale.

> *"That's right Alexandra; our car does have the features you are looking for. We are very proud that we have the only vehicle in its class to get over 20 miles per gallon, and the 6-inch GPS screen is the largest in the industry."*

By telling the prospect what she wants to hear, the salesperson is confirming, which is good. But it's not what the prospect needs at this point. Telling or confirming makes the salesperson feel good, but it doesn't really help the sale.

When you use the Ask/Tell tool, prospects validate their own opinions. They are looking for validation. They are trying to take ownership. They are trying to make a decision. And once that happens, well, they get it!

> **Ask:** *"So Alexandra, what you are saying is that the 21 miles per gallon is important to you, and so is the size of the GPS screen. Why?"*
> *"Well, I am trying to keep my gas bill down to $100 a month, and anything over 20 miles per gallon will do that for me. As for the GPS screen, I just got reading glasses and I don't really want to get them out to use the system. The bigger screen means I can use it more often."*
> *"So these two features, the 21 miles per gallon and the GPS screen size are important to you?"*

> "They are now. I knew I wanted 20 miles per gallon in
> the new car, but I didn't realize what the 6-inch screen size
> means to me. It's an A priority now."
>
> **Tell:** "Well Alexandra, we have both of those features."

If the salesperson had told Alexandra only that they had the
two things she was looking for, that would have confirmed for her
what she was looking for.

Confirm: To support or establish the certainty; verify;
to make firmer; strengthen.

By asking, and by using the Ask/Tell tool, the salesperson got
Alexandra to validate what she was looking for, and to assign that
validation to the car she is currently looking at.

Validate: To declare or make valid; to establish the
soundness of; corroborate.

Confirming and validating may be the same to you, but to
your prospect, they are very different. She can transfer that ownership to another vehicle that gets 21 miles per gallon and has a
6-inch GPS screen, but the Law of First kicks in.

THE LAW OF FIRST

You always remember your first love, your first car, the first man
on the moon. Being first gets buyers to assign a value to your
solution that they believe comes only with the first solution.
It's why buyers have brand loyalty. They used it first.

Use the Ask/Tell tool when you need to transfer ownership.
Avoid the temptation to sell and push when the prospect "gets" a
feature of what you are selling. You can get very excited when a

prospect first gets it. All that time trying to explain what you do and how what you sell can work for them is finally coming to fruition!

Don't lose it now. Instead of just confirming, have the prospect validate. It will keep the focus and attention on the prospect, make him feel a sense of accomplishment, and attach these features to your solution.

> **"*Ask* when the prospect gets it, then validate with a *tell*."**

THE DIFFERENCE BETWEEN EDUCATION AND VALIDATION

So now you can use your understanding of asking and telling to help your prospect make a decision.

The structure of your sales call and how you use the Ask/Tell tool depends on your goals. Is your goal Education? Or is your goal Validation?

If your goal is to *educate,* you will set up your sales call one way. If it is to *validate,* you will set it up another. It all depends on your goal and what the buyer needs.

If your goal is to **EDUCATE,** then set it up to be educational. Plan your sales call in the normal educational way:

* Tell 'em what you are about to tell 'em.

* Tell 'em.

* Tell 'em what you have told 'em.

It's the classic education style and one we have adopted so well. There's time for an agreement before the meeting, and time for questions at the end, too. The structure of the call is to tell 'em, tell 'em, tell 'em.

Now, if you want to **VALIDATE,** you need to set the call up differently. You are trying to have the prospect confirm or validate. For a validate call, you would:

- Ask 'em what is important to them right now.

- Tell 'em what you can do.

- Ask 'em how would they use it/what would they do with it.

Using the Ask/Tell tool on a tactical level during a sales call is powerful. As you'll see, setting up the meeting with the tool works wonders as well.

MEETING SETUP

If the goal of the meeting is to EDUCATE...

Tell 'em	Introduction and agenda review	10-20% of the meeting
Tell 'em	What you do and two-way education	60-80% of the meeting
Tell 'em	What you told them and next steps	10-30% of the meeting

If the goal of the meeting is to VALIDATE...

Ask 'em	What have they seen so far/use it for	30-50% of the meeting
Tell 'em	You can do it	10-20% of the meeting
Ask 'em	How would they use it and next steps	20-50% of the meeting

---

It really is that simple. Ask/Tell is a great tactical tool to find out what is really going on.

J.P. Morgan said,

"A person usually has two reasons for doing something.
One that sounds good, and a real reason."

The real reason needs to be uncovered on every sales call. You can use Ask/Tell to get the prospect to state that they...

"Get it!"

Ask/Tell^{Tool}

VEA Worksheet

Ask = Confirm: "Is this what you said?"

Tell = Validate: "Yes, we have what you are looking for."

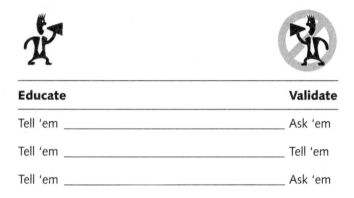

Educate		Validate
Tell 'em _____		Ask 'em
Tell 'em _____		Tell 'em
Tell 'em _____		Ask 'em

How are you going to set up your next meeting?

_____

_____

_____

What specifically are you going to do?

_____

_____

_____

Ask/Tell^{Tool}
TakeAways

1. What did you learn from this tool?

   _____

   _____

   _____

2. What prospect will you use this tool with? In what way?

   _____

   _____

   _____

3. Which people or partners will you share this tool with?
   What will you tell them?

   _____

   _____

   _____

4. What will you change based on using this tool?

   _____

   _____

   _____

PART THREE

The End

"I can get them all the way to the close. Then I don't know what happens...they just seem to delay and delay."

"I feel in control until I hand them my proposal. Then it seems like all I do is wait."

"Closing skills, that's what I need. I am tired of always having to do a deal to get a piece of business."

The end of the sale is the best part of the sale. That's when all your hard work comes to fruition. You've spent hours on this deal, and it is now time for the prospect to make a decision. You feel you have done all the work, everything the prospect asked for. You're ready to close.

Your prospect, however, doesn't share your enthusiasm. Prospects don't like to be closed. Would you liked to be closed? Prospects want to make a decision, either yes or no. How you set this up, how you make it easy for a prospect to make a buy decision, that's what your job is!

Forget about closing skills for a moment. The thought of being closed is very one-directional. Closing is what you are going to do to someone, and most people do not like things done to them. They want to feel in control.

So, instead of trying to make prospects feel out of control while you "close" them, here are some tools for you to help them make a buy decision. If you have done all the right things up until this point, the odds are in your favor that you will win more than you lose. After all, that's the way sales is (and hopefully you win a lot more than you lose).

The tools in this part of the *Tool Kit* are here for you to assist the prospect in making a decision. Some are to be used on almost every sales call. Some are for only when you need them. You will find these tools will help you reinforce your prospect's buying decision rather than put you in a position where you have to come up with a deal to close the sale. The tools here are:

- Summarize/Bridge and Pull^{Tool}
- TimeDemo^{Tool}
- I-Date^{Tool}
- Homework Assignment^{Tool}
- Neutral Elements^{Tool}

Have these tools ready to use at the end of the sale. Isn't it always at the end of the home-repair project when you realize you're missing an important tool and have to make a last-minute run to the hardware store? If you'd had that final tool—the right tool at the right time—you would have finished the job sooner. It's a heck of a lot easier when you have the right tool at the right time. So here you go: the final tools to help your prospect make a decision.

Summarize/Bridge and Pull^{Tool}

Tool Kit

**Summarize/Bridge and Pull^{Tool}: How to end every sales call
                                    with you in control of the
                                    sale.**

How can I finish strong at the end of a call? • How do I stay
in control? • What can I do when the prospect wants to go
in one direction and I want to go in another? • How do I get
back in control of a sale that is going nowhere?

How do you stay in control at the end of each sales call and at the
end of each sale? There are three things to keep in mind when you
are planning the end of a sales call. (You do plan for the end,
right?)

131

1. *It's your attitude.* You are in control of this sale. This is not the time to have the prospect take control. It's your sale and buyers want to be led, so you should have the attitude that they are expecting you to take the lead. After all, you are a salesperson in charge of a sale. So lead! Know what you want as a final outcome for this sales call before the sales call starts. Ask yourself:

> If all goes well on this call today, I would expect the next step to be_____.

   Or you can just wing it. Come on, use the tools and be prepared on every call.

2. *It's your direction.* You have been leading this sale the entire time. You should know the next buying step and be ready to propose it.

3. *It's your ending.* Use the tool to stay in control of each step and at the end of the sale. Most salespeople start off the call with the beginning in mind. But great sales calls start with the end in mind.

Summarize/Bridge and Pull (SBP) is a tool that you use at every step in the sale. And it's how you should end every call. Every call has to end with an SBP. Here is an example:

> "Well Mr. Henry, it sounds like we covered quite a lot today and had a good meeting. Let's review.
>
> "You said you wanted to lower your costs up to 15 percent by better managing your sales costs and increasing your lead generation capability. We discussed how we might be able to help you do this. (Summarize) Would you agree?" (Bridge)
>
> **Prospect:** "Yes, we did. It has been a good meeting all the way around."

> **You:** "That's great. So it sounds like a good next step should be where we both sit down, dig a little deeper into what we do, and how you could use it, and at that point you'll be in a perfect position to determine if we should go any further. Does that sound good to you?" (Pull)

This is a well-executed SBP. By looking at the structure, you can see how simple yet powerful this tool is.

A well-executed SBP has three parts. They are:

1. Them/You

2. Agree?/Bridge

3. Next Step

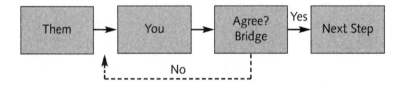

Them/You

When you want to end a sales call, you summarize the discussion you just completed and make sure you put the prospect's position first. Start with an introduction statement, and then go right for a Them/You position statement.

> "Well, Mr. Henry, it sounds like we covered quite a lot today and had a good meeting. Let's review. You said you wanted to lower your costs up to 15 percent by better managing your sales costs and increasing your lead generation capability. We discussed how we might be able to help you do this.

Agree?/Bridge

Here is where salespeople prepare prospects to go across the bridge with them. This is not losing control, since you are the one proposing the bridge. Ask the prospect if he is ready to go across a bridge.

> "Would you agree?"

Usually the buyer agrees, since it is a summation of the conversation that just took place. All he is agreeing to is that he said this and you said that. It sounds pretty good right now. You need to get this agreement to make sure all parties are on the same page. In some cases prospects may hesitate or not agree. This is good, since you will uncover an objection, hidden or otherwise, that must be dealt with and dealt with early.

If the prospect has no objections, hidden or otherwise, Bridge to the next step.

Next Step

This is when you propose the next step in the buy/sales process.

> "That's great. So it sounds like a good next step should be where we both sit down and dig a little deeper into what we do and how you could use it. At that point, you'll be in a perfect position to determine if we should go any further. Does that sound good to you?"

Again, in most cases, the prospect will agree since it is a natural next step in the buying process. You have completed your SBP and you are in control of this deal.

An SBP should be done at every meeting and after every conversation. It's easy to lose control of a deal, especially at the end.

Ending a sales call is always a battle for control. When you're fighting that battle, an SBP tool will help you stay one step ahead.

Sometimes, the prospect will jump right in and propose a next step.

> "So Mr. Henry, I think we have covered quite a bit and it sounds like we may be able to help you with the situation you were describing."
>
> *"Yes, what you have sounds interesting. Why don't you call Kami Mowbrey, my sales operations manager, and run this by her."*

This is pretty good. You are talking to a senior person, they have told you what to do and who to go to, and because you want to please and you want to get the sale, you actually are considering doing what they ask you to do.

 This is a battle for control, and if you do what they tell you to do, you will always be taking orders, especially if it is not what you think is the next step. Stay in control. If it is not what you want to do, then say so.

> "So Mr. Henry, I think we have covered quite a bit and it sounds like we may be able to help you with the situation you were describing."
>
> *"Yes, what you have sounds interesting. Why don't you call Kami Mowbrey, my sales operations manager, and run this by her."*
>
> "That sounds great. However, first, before we do that, I'm thinking a good next step for us to take, based on what we just talked about is xxxxx, and then, if that is okay with you, we can proceed to a next step that would be of benefit to Ms. Mowbrey."

However you want to phrase it is up to you, but this is all about sales call control, and don't lose it. Not staying in control here is putting you in a reactive sales position, where you will be following someone else's lead. Then you become commoditized, not a good position to be in. If it is a step that you need to take, agree, but then propose your next step.

> "So Mr. Henry, I think we have covered quite a bit and it sounds like we may be able to help you with the situation you were describing."
>
> "Yes, what you have sounds interesting. Why don't you call Kami Mowbrey, my sales operations manager, and run this by her."
>
> "That sounds great. I'll do that, but then I also want to get back with you afterwards and go over the results, so at that point you'll be in a position to determine if we should do anything else." ("...Because there is no way I am getting off this phone call if you're in control of this sale!" is what you'd better be thinking.)
>
> "Sounds great."

Summarize/Bridge and Pull is a way to make sure you are in control at the end of every meeting. Many sales have been spoiled after salespeople left a meeting thinking they were in control when they were not.

Additional items on the use of this tool:

- Do not ask the prospect what to do next. You are in charge of this sale, and you should know what to do next. Buyers want to be led.

- It's okay to agree to the prospect's requested next step. Just don't end there. At the end of the call, make sure you offer your next step so you stay in control.

* Always use a bridge. You must walk the prospect across the bridge. To do that, ask permission to cross the bridge:

> Would you agree?
>
> Is this what you thought we covered today?
>
> Does this sound about right?
>
> Any questions?

Summarize/Bridge and Pull is a powerful tool in your tool kit. You will get to a point where you will feel strange if you start a meeting without knowing how you want it to end. SBP gives you this structure—and control.

STORY—SUMMARIZE/BRIDGE AND PULL

The meeting was going really well. It seemed better than expected. Every question I asked was the right one, and the prospect was excited that we had asked the questions they had been expecting. Almost too good to be true; and then it happened.

We were having such a good time, we lost track of it. The senior executive stood up and said, "I'm really sorry, but I have committed myself to another meeting in three minutes. I have to go."

He looked at me as if he expected me to offer him something. I was stuck. The choices in front of me were to go on about how we were going to help them or cover the rest of the presentation, since it was about 15 more minutes of slides and discussion. Neither one looked attractive, so I decided to stay in control and do an SBP on the senior executive.

"Mr. Forrester, let's quickly review. You said you wanted to increase production by 10 percent this year. You have to get the new factory up and running by year's end, and without systems support, that is all but impossible. We told you that we can get those systems up and running by November, so I think we have had a good meeting, would you agree?"

"Oh, this has been a great meeting, I would agree."

"Okay then, so it seems the next step is to put the final details together so you can execute an agreement by the end of the week. Would you agree?"

There was silence for about three seconds, which seemed like three hours. It happened so fast, I didn't even have time to think about it. Finally, he said,

"Well, it seems to be the solution. Get that agreement to me by Thursday, and I'll get it through. Any questions anyone? No? Okay, I have to run. Thanks."

That SBP kept me in control of the meeting and helped me with that deal—with the senior executive in the room. I can't tell you how many deals I have lost or have had to delay because the senior person in the room had to leave early.

Would I have gotten the order with this company without SBP? Yeah, probably, but weeks later...and I probably would have had to discount. Love that SBP!

Summarize/Bridge and Pull^{Tool}
VEA Worksheet

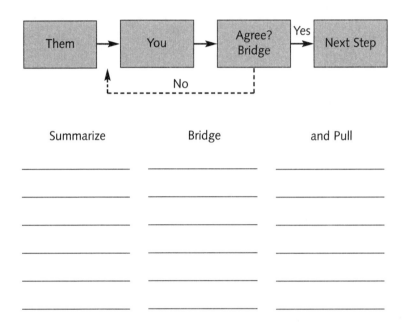

Summarize	Bridge	and Pull
_____	_____	_____
_____	_____	_____
_____	_____	_____
_____	_____	_____
_____	_____	_____
_____	_____	_____

Summarize/Bridge and Pull^{Tool}
TakeAways

1. What did you learn from this tool?

_____

_____

_____

2. What prospect will you use this tool with? In what way?

_____

_____

_____

3. Which people or partners will you share this tool with? What will you tell them?

_____

_____

_____

4. What will you change based on using this tool?

_____

_____

_____

TimeDemo^{Tool}

Tool Kit

TimeDemo^{Tool}: **How to create a sense of urgency so prospects
can overcome their fears and make decisions.**

How can I get the prospect over the fear of making a decision? •
What can I do to have the prospect make a decision about my sale?
• How can I get past delays and stalls and have the prospect, at
the highest levels, say, "Okay, let's do it."?

You have done a great job. The prospect has a proposal, she
knows what you are offering, and she knows where it fits in the
big picture. It's budgeted; everything looks good. So why isn't
she returning your calls?

Could be because you are selling something prospects do not
want to do, like to do, or appreciate having done for them. You are

asking a prospect to do something prospects HATE to do. Could be, you are asking the prospect to change.

"People hate to change."

Prospects are comfortable with how they are currently doing things, even though they know they have to change to stay ahead. If they are forced to change, they go kicking and screaming. They don't return your calls because they don't want to change in order to implement your ideas or to buy your products. They want to, but something is holding them back. It seems like it's a big investment, a big step forward, a huge risk. It's like jumping off a cliff.

Well jump off the cliff with them, with TimeDemo™.

TimeDemo is a tool to use with Russians—the revenue/cost crowd. It's a tool to use when you are near the end of the sale and you think the prospect is getting cold feet. It's for when they don't return your calls or they are evasive and noncommittal when you talk to them.

> "We still have some final touches we need to put on this one."
>
> "We are still trying to tie all the loose ends together."
>
> "Really, in a few more weeks, we'll be ready to proceed."

You have heard them all before. Use TimeDemo to take away some of that Fear of the Unknown, Fear of Failure, and (as Napoleon Hill calls it in *The Laws of Success*) Fear of Poverty. TimeDemo helps prospects overcome these fears and welcome change.

Fears drive decisions, either to completion or to delay. Even the fear of not making a decision is a powerful motivator. Lucky for you, fear is all in the mind. Oh, it's real, but it exists in the mind. You can use that little fact to help prospects overcome their fears. TimeDemo stretches out the fears and risks the prospect sees over time and makes those fears and risks seem more manageable and easier to deal with.

You know exactly what the prospect is going through with your proposal. He has arrived at a point in time when he has to make a decision.

"I wonder if we have looked at all the options."

"I don't know if this is the right time to spend this kind of money."

"It seems to me we need to make sure, really sure, this is the right thing to do, and that we are ready for it."

You could probably add one or two to the list above yourself. The prospect has stalled, he's nervous. The decision process has come to a head. A decision must be made. It better be a right, good, and fair one. And it better be profitable. It also has to be able to be implemented, measured, and bought into by everyone. Heck, with that much pressure, you wouldn't want to make a decision either. So stop looking at the decision as a point in time and try seeing it as a step.

If you start where the prospect is today, you need to take him through time in two steps. Step 1 is to start from today—and take him to Tomorrow, which is typically 30 to 60 days out. First, remind him where he is today and that he has a need. Then ask him how would he feel if he implemented your solution, or started using the item he is thinking about purchasing from you, or began to use your product or service, and what you sold him were doing what he expected it to do when he invested in it 30 to 60 days ago.

And if 30 to 60 days from now, the investment he made today was paying off well, how would he feel about that?

> "I'd feel great."
>
> "I'd feel relieved."
>
> "It would be really good."

You have moved the prospect away from the *fears* involved in making a decision. Now he has one set of feelings about today (which are not conducive to moving a decision forward) and another set of feelings about tomorrow. Tomorrow feels great, and the more he talks about it, the less today's fears will rear their ugly heads.

You don't want to stop. You have moved the prospect to the edge of the cliff, and so far so good. Now, have the prospect jump off the cliff. Have him do a TimeDemo. Move him to the next time area, which is about three to six months out, in an area called NEXT.

NEXT is a great, great place.

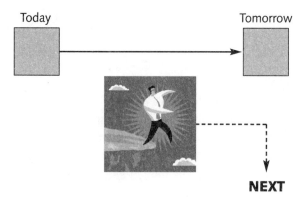

NEXT is where the prospect wants to be.

"It's where he'll find his Hopes, Dreams, and Desires."

> "So Mr. Berman, once you have our system up and running and things are going smoothly, what would you want to do next? What would be next for you and your team?"
>
> "Bob, after you have the product in production, which should be in about 30 days, what will you focus on next? What is it you want to do next?"

The prospect has now been moved through time and into the future—about three to six months into the future. At this point, your prospect says:

> "Next? For me? Well, I'll tell you what's next. Once this is up and running, I can start doing what I really want to do. I've really wanted to spend more time on..."

NEXT is indeed a great place. It's a place the prospect wants to be. Now your solution is seen as just one step in the process, rather than that big cliff you want them to jump off. TimeDemo lowers fears and minimizes risk.

> "Heck, this is just one step in the process to get to NEXT, and I need to get to next, so I need to take this step..."

A special note of caution: TimeDemo only works on decision makers. Decision makers have the vision and the strategy in place to know what's next. Lower-level people are waiting to be told what to do, so when you ask them what's next, they really can't tell you. After all, they haven't been told yet.

Using the tools at the decision maker's desk will result in a shorter sales cycle. Additionally, the prospect's desire to "get a good deal" has been minimized as well, since it is now just one step in the master plan. The focus on this BIG INVESTMENT has now been put into its proper perspective.

TimeDemo is a tool to get decision makers off the dime, put their fears to rest, and help them through the process of change. Prospects want and need to change. They just need some help jumping off that cliff.

TimeDemo^{Tool}

VEA Worksheet

Fill out a sales situation where you want to discuss TimeDemo with a prospect.

Today   Tomorrow

_____   _____

_____   _____

_____   _____

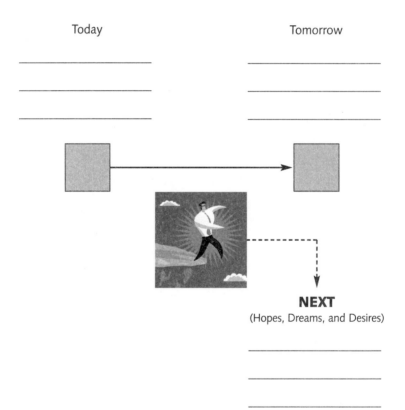

NEXT
(Hopes, Dreams, and Desires)

_____

_____

_____

TimeDemo^{Tool}

TakeAways

1. What did you learn from this tool?

_____

_____

_____

2. What prospect will you use this tool with? In what way?

_____

_____

_____

3. Which people or partners will you share this tool with?
   What will you tell them?

_____

_____

_____

4. What will you change based on using this tool?

_____

_____

_____

I-Date^{Tool}

Tool Kit

I-Date^{Tool}: **How to get the prospect to commit to a date. How to determine if you have a real sale or a maybe.**

Do I have a real qualified sale, or is it a waste of time? • How can I get the prospect to commit and not keep my deal from slipping? • What information is needed for me to make sure I have a deal worth spending time on?

    The maybe-buster.

    I-Date^{Tool}, or Implementation Date, is such a powerful tool, it's called the maybe-buster. A *maybe* from the customer is the worst answer you can get. If you get a yes from the prospect, that's great; you get an order. If you get a no, that's usually bad, but since you learn more from your losses than your victories, no's are not that bad either (unless, of course, you get a lot of them). When you get a no, you can fix whatever's wrong.

A maybe, which sounds like you still have a chance, is bad.

1. It freezes you. You cannot take any real action.
2. The prospect is in control. You have to wait to hear back.
3. You cannot go out and prospect since if this deal heats up, you are going to be real busy. (Who wants to go out and prospect when you have a maybe sitting in the funnel anyway? Ugh!)

There are two parts to the I-DateTool. The first is to know what date your prospect will begin using what you are trying to sell. The second part is to go hunting for dragons. Dragons and I-Dates are the maybe-busters.

Salespeople are under the impression that the sales-end date is just as important to the prospect as it is to them. Prospects think differently.

	Salespeople	**Prospect**
Key Date	End date	Start date
Final Step	Contract Sign	Start to use
Work Begins	Start of the sale	End of the sale
Work Ends	30 days after	When in use and fully functional

A salesperson cares when you buy the television. You care when that 60" LCD screen is up on the wall, all seven speakers are connected, and you are watching your first DVD. Prospects care about I-Dates, the start dates of the things they spend their money on. I-Dates are when changes begin to happen, when behavior shifts to new patterns.

The Prospect's Timeline View of How They Buy

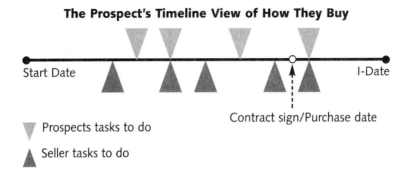

Start Date   I-Date

Contract sign/Purchase date

▽ Prospects tasks to do

▲ Seller tasks to do

What date does the prospect commit to when you ask:

> "What date are you going to start using...?"
>
> "What date will this go into production...?"
>
> "When are you going to take this home...?"
>
> "When do you need to have this delivered...?"

What date does the prospect commit to? By when does your proposed solution need to be up and running, on the dock, in production? At what date are they going to start getting their money back? What date is most important to the prospect—and it has to be the prospect's date, not yours. You can't offer a date and have the prospect agree to it. That would mean he's agreeing to your date, and not really thinking and committing to a date that fits his schedule.

All prospects have reasons for making changes. In fact, they're probably evaluating you to see if they want to include you in their change. Time is a valuable resource, so the prospect has to know how much time he wants to spend on a task such as evaluating your product or service. If there's a time frame (and there usually is), it probably has a start date and an end date.

A prospect's start date is driven by the end date. You may be considering a vacation, but until you decide when you are going, you're really just kicking tires. Once you have finished identifying when you are going on the vacation (I-Date), you have a reasonable idea of when you will begin planning, and you have a reasonable idea of when you will  finalize your plans. And all that planning centers on the I-Date.

Get the prospect's I-Date, make sure it's a firm date, and then go hunt for some dragons. Time to put on that armor and get some real fire-breathing dragons to make sure the I-Date is real.

DRAGONS

Dragons are what cause an I-Date to be firm. They are key events, commitments, promises, tasks, goals, and objectives that are tied to the I-Date. Examples of dragons are:

If You Are Selling	Possible Dragon
Information for a presentation	Board meeting
Cars	End of a lease
Tennis Rackets	Start of a tournament
Consulting Services	Launch of a new product
Televisions	Sporting Event

The list goes on and on. Every sale should have at least two to three dragons associated with it. This will give you confidence that the I-Date is firm, and you will get a yes or a no decision—not a maybe.

What a dragon is not:

* Hot buttons

* Pain points

* Go-to features

* Anything to do with what you are selling

What a dragons is:

* Something that is causing the prospect to seek education

* Some event or date they have committed to

* Some event or date their boss has committed to

* A promise made

* A Management Objective (MBO) they need to accomplish to get their pay

Something, anything that makes their calendar, has their attention. Something they need to take action on and have been procrastinating over.

Ask them about their dragons, not about your features and benefits. They are their dragons, and you have to get a complete description of the dragon to see what kind it is so you know if you can slay it.

Usually there is such demand for limited resources that prospects won't spend money unless they have a few dragons to satisfy. This will justify their spending money and will also get more people on their side—which spreads risk and increases the odds of a successful implementation.

The best dragons breathe fire. If you can find these, the I-Date has a very, very small chance of slipping.

Fire-breathing dragons are commitments that prospects have made to others—such as their bosses, co-workers, friends, or spouses. A commitment made to others so that they can get something they need is an even bigger fire-breathing dragon, since now there are really two dragons dependent on the I-Date!

Ask for prospect dragons, and if there are some, at least two, the chances of a maybe have gone way down.

STORY—THE LAPTOP

Bri was looking to buy a laptop computer. She had visited a few stores in search of a good deal on something that would meet her needs. Now she was down to two choices and was discussing the value of each one with the salesperson.

"I really can't decide between these two. I know all the features and the warranty information. I just can't decide."

"This is the third trip you have made to the store this week," said Kyle, the salesperson. "Let me ask you a question. Why do you need this laptop?"

"Well, my other one is getting old, and I was interested in getting a new one."

"Why now? What is causing you to look today?"

"I am starting a new job next Friday," said Bri. "And the projects I'll be working on will be big ones. So, I want a new computer that's faster than the one I have, and one with more memory."

At this point, many salespeople would launch into speed and storage discussions. But not our boy Kyle. Kyle's looking for the I-Date. He's looking for a few dragons.

"Okay, so next Friday is an important date. What else is making you look so hard right now?"

"Well," Bri explained, "I am going on a business trip on Monday, and won't be back until Thursday. This is really my last time to look. It's either now or hold off for a few more weeks."

Armed with two I-Dates, Kyle began discussing what was important to Bri—the dates, not the features.

"Okay, it seems you would like to have the new computer by next Friday, and since you will be traveling, the only day to get one would be today. Is that right?"

"Yeah, that's right," Bri agreed.

"Well, if you decided to get one now, you could take it on the trip with you," said Kyle. "And you could transfer your files before you leave, or even during the trip. That would give you a few days to get used to the new computer. So by Friday, you'd be up and running with the new laptop, and the learning curve would be behind you. You would be ready to give that first new project 100 percent of your attention. Is that right?"

You know the rest of the story. Kyle focused on the I-Date. He found the dragons, and then he used them to help Bri decide to get a new laptop in the time frame she said she needed. Heck of a lot better than feature/benefiting her to death with speed, storage size, screen resolution, and blah, blah, blah....

I-Date^{Tool}
VEA Worksheet

Dragons Timeline

▼ Start Date   I-Date

▼ Prospects tasks to do

Dragons the Prospect Needs to Work On:

1. _____ By what date?_____

2. _____ By what date?_____

3. _____ By what date?_____

4. _____ By what date?_____

5. _____ By what date?_____

Things or Commitments the Prospect Has to Do Right Now:

1. _____ By what date?_____

2. _____ By what date?_____

3. _____ By what date?_____

4. _____ By what date?_____

5. _____ By what date?_____

I-Date™ᵒᵒˡ
TakeAways

1. What did you learn from this tool?

   _____

   _____

   _____

2. What prospect will you use this tool with? In what way?

   _____

   _____

   _____

3. Which people or partners will you share this tool with? What will you tell them?

   _____

   _____

   _____

4. What will you change based on using this tool?

   _____

   _____

   _____

Homework Assignment^{Tool}

Tool Kit

Homework Assignment^{Tool}: The prospect needs to take ownership of the sale. Use this tool to get the prospect involved in your solution and create value.

What can I have the prospect do that will put my solution in the best light? • How can I add value to my solution and differentiate it from the competition? • What should I have the prospect do so we can work together on a solution?

Why do you think you should be doing all the work to get this sale? Yes, you are the salesperson, but if prospects don't get involved, they won't value the overall solution. You need to get your prospects involved, and not just with demonstrations. Give them things to do. They want to get involved. They really want something to do. So, give them a Homework Assignment.

You know that when the prospect is really involved in what you are selling, ownership transfers and the likelihood of a sale increases. Most times, this happens because the prospect starts taking over the sale and you get lucky. Other times, you set up a demonstration of what you do and hope that after the demo the prospect "gets it."

It's time to be proactive with that transfer of ownership step, and to give your prospects something to do to involve them in the sale!

Homework Assignments are tactics during the sale process that need to get accomplished. You do not need to give them something to do that has no value, or is something that you made up just to keep them busy. Prospects can smell if you are trying to give them something that is of no value, so keep Homework Assignments to something that has value to the buy/sell process. The idea is to involve the prospect in the sale.

Breaking Paradigms

Success with this tool requires you to break three paradigms:

1. You are the salesperson and you have to do everything yourself. This is the attitude of most salespeople, and it is flat wrong. If the prospect is the one who is going to be using what you are selling, doesn't it make sense to involve him in the sale? Prospects want to be involved. Heck, it's their money and their risk, so get them involved. Here are just a few tasks you can assign to your prospects:

* Have them write the proposal or work on the rough draft together.

* Let them give a demonstration of what or how they are going to use your solution.

* Give them the wipe board marker and have them open the meeting.

* Send a rough draft of the agenda and ask them to make additions or changes.

* Let them come up with options that may be useful. This usually is done when the prospect loves choice (control) and many options are available.

* Commit someone in their company to a phone call or a meeting and have them set it up.

* Dedicate someone from their team to work with you in creating a demonstration.

* Have them give you presentations on what they're looking for.

* Get a package of information on what the company does. This would include annual reports, sales brochures, or sample proposals—anything that will give you more insight into what your prospects do and how they will use your product.

2. The prospect is too busy to get involved. You are typically talking to the wrong person then. Senior managers, i.e., cost and revenue thinkers, know if they get their staff involved in the solution, their risk will be lowered, so they want to get their people involved. Isn't that why they have so many people working for them? Their people need something to do, something of value. Russians want to get their people involved, so let them.

It's the lower-level managers, the ones who will
be using your product who may complain that they
have too much work to do to take on a Homework
Assignment. At this point you should explain, in their
lingo, why a Homework Assignment is so important—
or find someone else to sell to.

3. You are out of control of this sale. You are in second,
    third, or last place, and the prospect just doesn't want to
    get you involved with "his" sale, since the chance he'll
    do business with you is pretty small. (If they don't want
    to try the shoes on, are they really qualified prospects?)

    Knowing this, you can either get back into control
    with a Homework Assignment: Stress that you can go
    no further unless what you are asking for gets done.
    Or, drop the prospect, since you are just not in a good
    competitive position.

    You have to give them something to do. If you
    don't, you are pushing—and hoping they get it.
    Why would you do that? A Homework Assignment
    contradicts this natural sales philosophy:

**"If I do all the work, I'll get the sale.
I really can't trust anyone else."**

It's time to get over that idea. The more control of the sale you
give up, the more control you really have. The more homework
you give out, the more they'll come back to you. After all, you are
the one who is developing the final solution. The person giving
out homework is the one in control, which is a thought you should
carry with you when you agree to do everything the prospect

needs to get done for this sale to happen. (Yep, you are giving up control.) Getting them involved in what they are buying gets them:

* Doing something sooner

* Finding more value

* Assuming less risk

* Spending less time with your competition

* Dedicating more time to the solution (which means more dragons!)

* Increasing the chance for a Win-Win solution

As we said, senior managers are more likely to take on homework assignments. It's normal for them. Lower-level managers are the ones who'll complain that they already have enough on their plates and can't take on additional work. Having heard that response so many times in the past, you may be reluctant to pull out this tool.

However, mid-level managers have resources. They have reports to whom they're just dying to assign some "valuable" work; "A-players" who want to try something new, something that will stretch them. Think of your situation: If your boss came to you and asked for your help on something new and different that could help the company, advance your career, or make you more money, you'd do it.

Cost and revenue decision makers are always looking for something to challenge their A-players, so why not help your prospect out? They like homework assignments, and so should you.

HOMEWORK ASSIGNMENT

A salesperson at a company that sells web-based meetings and collaboration tools tells an interesting story.

"I was working a sale with a vice president of sales. He wanted to use our solution to help his weekly sales meetings. The feature he liked best about our solution was the video function, where you can have the meeting attendees on the screen during the meeting, as long as each person at the web-meeting had a web cam. (A web cam is that little camera you can attach to your PC or laptop and see yourself when you plug it in.) The sale was moving along great, but I sensed they were not going to take advantage of the total solution. They really needed to take the solution offered. I knew of way too many customers who felt nervous about trying something new, then purchased less than the solution required, then had to upgrade way before they thought they needed to. That causes everyone headaches. It's best to buy the whole thing up front. With this in mind, I came up with a Homework Assignment idea.

"John," I said, "I know you have asked me for a final proposal, but I don't want to give you one yet. You really need to understand the solution we are offering, so what I would like you to do is go get a web cam. Go purchase a web cam, plug it in, use our demo software with it that you have, and see for yourself what we're talking about." It was a risky decision, but I knew what the right solution was for this company, and I did not want to give up without trying.

"The next morning at 8:10 a.m., my phone rings and it's this VP, telling me he went to the store last night, bought a web cam, plugged it into his laptop at home, and was amazed at what he could do with it. He went on and on about how he could use it for this meeting and that meeting. He was so excited, he was selling me on the deal, and I even learned something new about web cams. He signed the deal that day, and has been one happy customer, and a great reference ever since. "

The bottom line is: The more you get them involved, the more control you have, the more they understand the solution, and the more benefit everyone gets. Give up that control and win more deals. Okay, who is going to write that next proposal?

Here is a list of possible Homework Assignments. Be sure to have a list like this on the wall in your office or by the phone. Take it with you on sales calls.

Homework Assignment^{Tool}
VEA Worksheet

Assignment	Complete?
Proposal	_____
Joint price list	_____
Prospect demo	_____
Prospect care kit	_____
Prospect care package	_____
Factory tour	_____
Having them check with someone who is a peer or a superior.	_____
Submit a list of people to you that you can call	_____
Send you an e-mail	_____
_____	_____
_____	_____
_____	_____
_____	_____
_____	_____

Homework Assignment^{Tool}
TakeAways

1. What did you learn from this tool?

_____

_____

_____

2. What prospect will you use this tool with? In what way?

_____

_____

_____

3. Which people or partners will you share this tool with? What will you tell them?

_____

_____

_____

4. What will you change based on using this tool?

_____

_____

_____

Neutral Elements^{Tool}

Tool Kit

Neutral Elements^{Tool}: **A prospect-communication tool that gets all parties involved and helps everyone understand the different points of view, without you pushing.**

Do I have a real qualified sale, or is it a waste of time? • How can I get the prospect to commit and to keep my deals from slipping? • What information do I need to help me know if this deal is worth my time?

Have you been there? Have you been on that sales call where try as you may, you just don't get what the prospect is trying to tell you, and your clarification questions are being met with looks like you are selling bad lemons.

Worse, have you had the sales call where you were eloquent in your description of the solution and all the benefits the prospect would get once she makes a decision, only to be met with that same lemony look?

Sometimes both parties are trying to say something, but there's no happy meeting ground, no place where each party can express itself so that the other party can understand. Sound confusing? Here come Neutral Elements.

One problem with sales calls is the enormous amount of subjectivity flying around during conversations. When two parties get together, the conversation tends to go back and forth. The more back and forth it goes, the more subjective it gets—and the less clear and meaningful it becomes.

LARRY (THE SALESPERSON): So what I hear you say is you want the software additions as well as the maintenance program for three years, right?

DONNA (THE PROSPECT): Not exactly. I need you to understand how the process works.

LARRY: Okay, please tell me again.

DONNA: Larry, here is a flow chart of our current system, and as you can see...

The flow chart becomes a Neutral Element, a document, picture, or diagram that each party can refer to when discussing what the other needs to understand. All the parties take ownership of Neutral Elements, recognizing them as real and true. Each party wants the other to agree, modify, understand, or change so they can reach an agreement.

You have been in those meetings when you need to draw pictures on a wipe board for everyone to understand what you are talking about. That's a Neutral Element. Not the wipe board, but the picture, flow chart, diagram, whatever you write on it. Remember, a picture is worth a thousand words, and when you use a Neutral Element that both parties can reference, you are helping the transfer of ownership.

Why do you think salespeople at high-end clothing stores follow you into the dressing room area? It's not that they want to hang out there, since most of the potential customers are out in the store. They follow you in for the use of a Neutral Element: your reflection in a mirror.

Did you ever notice that successful clothing salespeople will send you into the dressing room to try on the clothes, and when you emerge, you and the salesperson are discussing the articles of clothing you are thinking about buying—and you're both looking in the mirror? It's your reflection that you're talking about, not you! The salesperson goes on and on about how well the garment hangs or fits. He's talking about you, but it's as if you were detached from your own body.

> "Yes, you look great in this. See where it fits you great in the shoulder?"
>
> "Yes, I agree. Do you think this style makes my neck look too big?"
>
> "What? Of course not. Look here. You can see where the top fits perfectly around the neck and shoulders..." (Notice it's the neck and shoulders, not your neck and shoulders.)
>
> "You are right; and look at the way it goes across the body."

It's almost as though you don't exist. Imagine the salesperson trying to have the same conversation and you not being able to see yourself as the salesperson sees you. You would be twisting around and having an awkward time trying to see yourself. Increased frustration means less sales opportunity, which is why they talk to mirrors.

Other ideas for Neutral Elements include:

- Wipe boards
- Pen and paper
- Brochures
- Working illustrations
- Diagrams
- Pictures
- Forms
- Rough draft quotes
- Manuals

To be effective with this tool, remember: It is not what you use; it's how you use it.

The Neutral Element Rules

- A Neutral Element is an item to propel a mutual conversation.
- It is not something you give someone so that they can review it.
- Worse, it is not something you send someone and hope they understand.
- You can only send it to someone if you are going to use it as a mutual discussion piece.

* The more involved the prospect gets; the better.
  It should be something prospects can write on, point to,
  fill out, make reference to, or use otherwise.

* The more you can use a Neutral Element from scratch,
  the better. If the picture is complete or the form is
  already filled out, the prospect has to catch up, and
  then communication is one way.

When someone has an interest in what we do, on the first sales call, I send them an agenda. Now this is not a normal agenda. This agenda has about 12 items on it, and it gives the prospect options. I ask prospects to check off the three or four areas where they have the most interest, so I can tailor the presentation to their needs. I always get back a checked form, and usually the prospect brings the form they filled out to the meeting.

When I talk to prospects for the first time, I pretty much know what they need to hear. I sent the agenda out for their benefit, not mine. I am rarely surprised by what the prospect checks, and rarely change my presentation. If it does come back with a "surprise," you can bet I am on the phone with the prospect before the meeting to make sure I fully understand what was meant by that checkmark that surprised me.

We call this a Prospective Agenda for a reason. It tells me what to prepare for; it gets prospects involved. And because they're involved, transfer of ownership has already begun. Now, that's Neutral Elements at work before the first meeting. Nice!

So how long do you think it would take to send this out in an e-mail attachment? Not only is it a Neutral Element, it is also a Homework Assignment.

AGENDA

Thank you for our discussion today. In preparation for our meeting, please check three or four primary areas of interest so we can tailor our presentation to answer the questions you may have up front. This will maximize your time and involvement. Please bring this to the meeting.

Areas of interest you may have:

- Overall capabilities
- Specific to engineering
- Specific to finance
- How you would start using it
- How to get support
- How this integrates with your current operation
- Typical costs
- Other user examples
- Our company
- Typical investigation process
- Detailed specifications
- Typical installation examples

Thank You,
Sales Representative
The ABC Company

The agenda above is a real example, and the salesperson who thought it up uses it to kick off the meeting. It gets the prospect talking right up front and starts the meeting off on the right foot.

"They start talking about their issues and concerns, and it gives me time to really understand what they are looking for. Half the time, we don't even get into the presentation; we're just discussing what they want and how we can help them. Pretty cool."

It is so easy to want to give: You give your presentation, your brochure, your demonstration. You give everything in hope that if the prospect gets this information, he will be convinced you are the answer.

Prospects don't buy that way. How they will use your product or service has to be their idea. So, get your prospects involved before and during the meeting with Neutral Elements.

Neutral Elements^{Tool}
VEA Worksheet

Agenda

Thank you for our discussion today. In preparation for our meeting, please check three or four primary areas of interest so we can tailor our presentation to answer the questions you may have right up front and maximize your time and involvement. Please bring this to the meeting.

Areas of interest you may have:

_____

_____

_____

_____

_____

_____

_____

_____

_____

_____

Thank You,
Sales Representative

Neutral Elements^{Tool}
TakeAways

1. What did you learn from this tool?

   _____

   _____

   _____

2. What prospect will you use this tool with? In what way?

   _____

   _____

   _____

3. Which people or partners will you share this tool with?
   What will you tell them?

   _____

   _____

   _____

4. What will you change based on using this tool?

   _____

   _____

   _____

E P I L O G U E

> "I have to get better every day."
>
> "I wouldn't take my family to a doctor who was winging it. Why is selling any different?"
>
> "I need more tools to use during the sales call. The ones I have I am very good at, but I need more."

These are quotes we get all the time when we are training salespeople. The goal is not to teach you a new way of selling. The goal is to give you more tools for your tool kit, and to have a handy reference guide that you can take with you on a sales call, or at least when you're preparing for a call. You know you are adding tools to your sales competence tool kit when:

- You start using the tools by name. "I have to practice my Summarize/Bridge and Pull" or "Let's do a TimeZone on that sales call tomorrow." The more you use the tool name, the more proficient you will become. Go to our website (www.m3learning.com) and download the list of tools in the Ultimate Tool Kit section.

- Share with a co-worker. The more you practice, the better you'll get. You would never ski or scuba dive alone. Same with the tools. It's always more fun working out with a partner.

- Other salespeople start coming to you for advice, and you just don't give your "opinion," you share a tool (and do so using Neutral Elements!).

I have been doing this for more than 10 years, for tens of thousands of salespeople and hundreds of companies. Working with the best, the A players is our goal. A players are not necessarily the ones with the highest quota, the top percent of quota, or the largest revenue producers (although they usually are). A players are the ones who give it their all, the ones who put it out there every day.

The A player is you. You may be the new rookie or the seasoned veteran; the one with the largest territory or maybe a follow-up salesperson. You are the one who is out there every day, listening to your customers and helping them get better value.

You, the A player, will use these tools. And you'll challenge yourself to come up with new tools. The tools in this book are the ones you told us work well. So thanks!

"Use the tools."

List of Tools

BuyThink^{Tool}: Think like a buyer and get buyers involved in their buying process.

- How would you want to be sold to?
- What information must you have in order to make a decision?
- How do you picture an ideal salesperson selling to you?
- Can you think like a buyer and be better prepared to launch a sales call?

PowerHour^{Tool}: Successful time management tool in one hour a day.

- How do I find great prospects?
- When can I call them?
- When should I focus my best efforts?

- How do I make sure I spend the right amount of time on the right prospects?
- Where do I get a few more hours in a day?

30-Second Intro^{Tool}: How to start a sales call.
- How do I get a sales call off on the right foot?
- How do I get the prospect to believe I can help him?
- How do I make sure prospects get interested and start talking with me, showing me, and explaining to me how they want to buy?

20-Second Intro^{Tool}: What an effective voice-mail or e-mail should look like to have the best chance of success.
- How do I leave an effective message so they call me back?
- Can I use e-mail to start a sales process?
- How can I quickly get someone's attention when they have little or no time?

3-Languages^{Tool}: How to speak the right language on every sales call and appeal to everyone's interest.
- When I am making a sales call, it's as though everyone I talk to speaks a different language.
- How do I know the right language to speak to the right person?
- When I am calling at the executive level, what do I say?

RePhrase+^{Tool}: Buyers want to make sure they are heard and understood.
- How do I make sure the prospect is really in agreement with what I am saying?

- How can I get the customer to say those magical words, "Yes, that's exactly what I need!"?

TimeZones^{Tool}: Buyers purchase to satisfy needs; and time considerations are a critical, deciding element.

- How can I create a sense of urgency with my prospect?
- How do I understand what time sensitive issues are really driving this buying decision?
- What do I need to know about the prospect's timing?

Yes, We Can Do That^{Tool}: Prospects want to feel their needs are being met. They want to feel like they are being heard.

- How can I get the buyer to understand that I really get what his needs are?
- Is there a way I can be in real rapport with the prospect?
- How much value is added by having the prospect believe that I understand his problem the best?

ValueStar^{Tool}: How prospects value and evaluate every solution—in their financial terms.

- How can I get the prospect to value what I am selling?
- Are how he values a solution and how I present value two different things?
- When it really matters, how do senior executives actually evaluate their return on a proposed solution?

3 Stages of Value^{Tool}: Buyers must quantitatively substantiate value in their own mind, and they need help getting there.

- How can I get the prospect to take ownership of the proposed solution?
- What are some great questions to help the prospect see the value?

Ask/Tell^{Tool}: Buyers want to be educated and have their decisions validated.

- How can I make sure the prospect is educated?
- How can I make sure the prospect really "gets it"?
- Is there a way to induce the transfer of ownership proactively?

Summarize/Bridge and Pull^{Tool}: How to end every sales call with you in control of the sale.

- How can I finish strong at the end of a call?
- How do I stay in control?
- What can I do when the prospect wants to go in one direction and I want to go in another?
- How do I get back in control of a sale that is going nowhere?

TimeDemo^{Tool}: How to create a sense of urgency so prospects can overcome their fears and make decisions.

- How can I get the prospect over the fear of making a decision?
- What can I do to have the prospect make a decision about my sale?
- How can I get past delays and stalls and have the prospect, at the highest levels, say, "Okay, let's do it."?

I-Date^{Tool}: How to get the prospect to commit to a date. How to determine if you have a real sale or a maybe.

- Do I have a real qualified sale, or is it a waste of time?
- How can I get the prospect to commit and not keep my deal from slipping?

- What information is needed for me to make sure I have a deal worth spending time on?

Homework Assignment^{Tool}: The prospect needs to take ownership of the sale. Use this tool to get the prospect involved in your solution and create value.

- What can I have the prospect do that will put my solution in the best light?
- How can I add value to my solution and differentiate it from the competition?
- What should I have the prospect do so we can work together on a solution?

Neutral Elements^{Tool}: A prospect communication tool that gets all parties involved and helps everyone understand the different points of view, without you pushing.

- Do I have a real qualified sale, or is it a waste of time?
- How can I get the prospect to commit and to keep my deals from slipping?
- What information do I need to help me know if this deal is worth my time?

List of Visual Exercise Areas (VEAs)

The Process^{Tool}
VEA Worksheet

Initiate: _____

_____

_____

Educate: _____

_____

_____

Justify: _____

_____

_____

Validate: _____

_____

_____

Close: _____

_____

_____

BuyThink™ool
VEA Solution Box

Your View of the Solution You Think the Prospect Wants

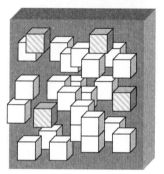

Solution Value to Prospect = $1.0m

Your Prospect's View of His Own Needs.

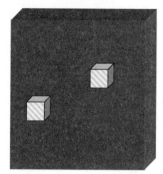

Solution Value to Prospect = $30m

The prospect's IQs:

_____

_____

The prospect's DOs:

_____

_____

Step on the GAS by:

_____

_____

PowerHour^{Tool}
VEA Worksheet

The account I am focusing on right now.

Whale: _____

Initial Contact Made: _____ ❑ ❑ ❑

Homework Level 1: _____ ❑ ❑ ❑

Homework Level 2: _____ ❑ ❑ ❑

E-Mail Sent: _____ ❑ ❑ ❑

E-Mail Sent: _____ ❑ ❑ ❑

E-Mail Sent: _____ ❑ ❑ ❑

E-Mail Sent: _____ ❑ ❑ ❑

Voice-Mail: _____ ❑ ❑ ❑

Presentation: _____ ❑ ❑ ❑

Presentation: _____ ❑ ❑ ❑

Sent Info: _____ ❑ ❑ ❑

Special note on using the PowerHour VEA Worksheet: The power of three is well documented, so on the PowerHour VEA Worksheet, you will notice three boxes on each line. Cross off each box each time you accomplish one of the line's goals. Then you can track your own progress.

30-Second Intro^{Tool}
VEA Worksheet

Introduction:

_____

_____

_____

3/:

    1. _____

    2. _____

    3. _____

Bridge: _____

/3:

    1. _____

    2. _____

    3. _____

Summarize and Flip: _____

_____

_____

20-Second Intro^{Tool}
VEA Pattern Interrupt Version

Introduction:

_____

_____

Pattern Interrupt:

"The purpose for my call is to answer any questions you may have regarding...

1. _____

2. _____

3. _____

Call to Action:

_____

_____

_____

20-Second Intro^{Tool}
VEA Help Version

Introduction:

   "Mr. XXXX, I'm _____ and could use your help..."

_____

_____

_____

Help:

   "I've been looking at your company, and there are a few questions I hope you can answer."

   Your Help Statement/Questions:

   1. _____

   2. _____

   3. _____

Call to Action:

_____

_____

_____

3-Languages^{Tool}
VEA Worksheet

Greek

Russian

Spanish

What question would you ask each type of prospect?

Spanish Questions:

_____

_____

_____

Russian Questions:

_____

_____

_____

Greek Questions:

_____

_____

_____

RePhrase+[Tool]
VEA Worksheet

You need to spend time on this exercise to get this tool, so fill in the blanks.

Spoken need by the prospect:

_____

_____

_____

What you would usually say:

_____

_____

_____

RePhrase:

_____

_____

_____

RePhrase+:

_____

_____

_____

TimeZones^{Tool}

VEA Worksheet

Who are you talking to and what is important to them?

Who and What

_____

_____

_____

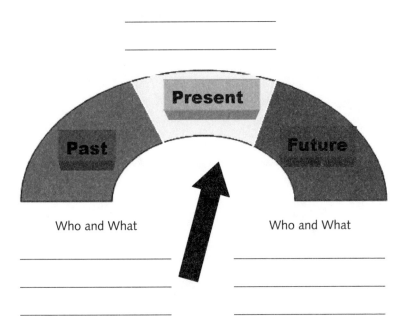

Who and What   Who and What

_____   _____

_____   _____

_____   _____

Yes, We Can Do That^{Tool}
VEA Worksheet

Xerox this page, and place it on your wall, right by your phone.

ValueStar™Tool
VEA Worksheet

List at least three concerns and issues your prospect has under each topic. This is not about you; it's about what your prospect has a problem with and her or his search for someone or something to solve it.

Risk

_____

_____

_____

ROI   Time

_____   _____

_____   _____

_____   _____

Brand   Leverage

_____   _____

_____   _____

_____   _____

3 Stages of Value^{Tool}
VEA Worksheet

Prospect's Three Stages of Value

Stage 1—Basic Understanding:

_____

_____

_____

Stage 2—Taking Ownership:

_____

_____

_____

Stage 3—Applying Value:

_____

_____

_____

3 Stages of Value^{Tool}
VEA Worksheet

Seller's Three Stages of Value

Stage 1—Agreement:

_____

_____

_____

Stage 2—Transfer of Ownership—HOW:

_____

_____

_____

Stage 3—Quantifying Value—WHAT:

_____

_____

_____

Ask/Tell^{Tool}
VEA Worksheet

Ask = Confirm: "Is this what you said?"

Tell = Validate: "Yes, we have what you are looking for."

Educate		Validate
Tell 'em _____		Ask 'em
Tell 'em _____		Tell 'em
Tell 'em _____		Ask 'em

How are you going to set up your next meeting?

_____

_____

_____

What specifically are you going to do?

_____

_____

_____

Summarize/Bridge and Pull^{Tool}
VEA Worksheet

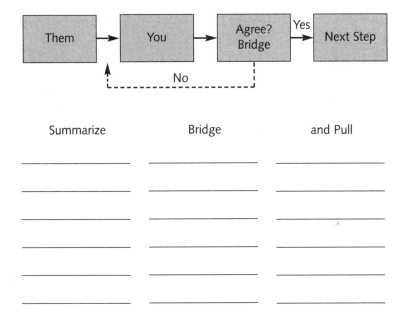

Summarize	Bridge	and Pull
_____	_____	_____
_____	_____	_____
_____	_____	_____
_____	_____	_____
_____	_____	_____
_____	_____	_____

TimeDemo^{Tool}
VEA Worksheet

Fill out a sales situation where you want to discussion TimeDemo with a prospect.

Today   Tomorrow

_____   _____

_____   _____

_____   _____

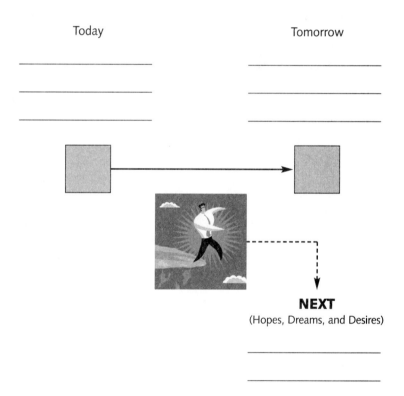

NEXT
(Hopes, Dreams, and Desires)

_____

_____

_____

I-Date^{Tool}
VEA Worksheet

Dragons Timeline

Start Date   I-Date

▼ Prospects tasks to do

Dragons the Prospect Needs to Work On:

1. _____ By what date?_____

2. _____ By what date?_____

3. _____ By what date?_____

4. _____ By what date?_____

5. _____ By what date?_____

Things or Commitments the Prospect Has to Do Right Now:

1. _____ By what date?_____

2. _____ By what date?_____

3. _____ By what date?_____

4. _____ By what date?_____

5. _____ By what date?_____

Homework Assignment^{Tool}
VEA Worksheet

Assignment	Complete?
Proposal	_____
Joint price list	_____
Prospect demo	_____
Prospect care kit	_____
Prospect care package	_____
Factory tour	_____
Having them check with someone who is a peer or a superior.	_____
Submit a list of people to you that you can call	_____
Send you an e-mail	_____
_____	_____
_____	_____
_____	_____
_____	_____
_____	_____

Neutral Elements™

VEA Worksheet

Agenda

Thank you for our discussion today. In preparation for our meeting, please check three or four primary areas of interest so we can tailor our presentation to answer the questions you may have right up front and maximize your time and involvement. Please bring this to the meeting.

Areas of interest you may have:

_____

_____

_____

_____

_____

_____

_____

_____

_____

_____

Thank You,
Sales Representative

C

Monthly Calendar of Tool Usage

Use the following pages to plan what tool to use during that week, and to keep a record of tools which you use. Be honest and keep a record. Copy the calendar and put it up on your wall. Use it daily.

January
Tools Review

PowerHour

30-Second Intro

Summarize/Bridge and Pull

Sunday	Monday	Tuesday	Wednesday	Thursday	Friday	Saturday
			1 PH, 30	2 PH, 30	3 SBP, 30	4
5	6	7 30, SBP	8	9 PH, SBP	10 PH, 30, SBP	11
12	13	14	15 PH, 30, SBP	16 PH, 30, RePh+	17	18
19	20	21 PH, 30, Yes, we	22	23	24	25
26	27	28	28	30	31	

January
Tools Review

This Month's Tools

_____

_____

_____

_____

Sunday	Monday	Tuesday	Wednesday	Thursday	Friday	Saturday

February
Tools Review

This Month's Tools

_____

_____

_____

_____

Sunday	Monday	Tuesday	Wednesday	Thursday	Friday	Saturday

March
Tools Review

This Month's Tools

_____

_____

_____

_____

Sunday	Monday	Tuesday	Wednesday	Thursday	Friday	Saturday

April
Tools Review

This Month's Tools

_____

_____

_____

_____

Sunday	Monday	Tuesday	Wednesday	Thursday	Friday	Saturday

May
Tools Review

This Month's Tools

_____

_____

_____

_____

Sunday	Monday	Tuesday	Wednesday	Thursday	Friday	Saturday

June
Tools Review

This Month's Tools

Sunday	Monday	Tuesday	Wednesday	Thursday	Friday	Saturday

July
Tools Review

This Month's Tools

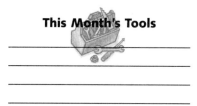

_____

_____

_____

_____

Sunday	Monday	Tuesday	Wednesday	Thursday	Friday	Saturday

August
Tools Review

This Month's Tools

_____

_____

_____

_____

Sunday	Monday	Tuesday	Wednesday	Thursday	Friday	Saturday

September
Tools Review

This Month's Tools

_____

_____

_____

_____

Sunday	Monday	Tuesday	Wednesday	Thursday	Friday	Saturday

October
Tools Review

This Month's Tools

_____

_____

_____

_____

Sunday	Monday	Tuesday	Wednesday	Thursday	Friday	Saturday

November
Tools Review

This Month's Tools

Sunday	Monday	Tuesday	Wednesday	Thursday	Friday	Saturday

December
Tools Review

This Month's Tools

_____

_____

_____

_____

Sunday	Monday	Tuesday	Wednesday	Thursday	Friday	Saturday

I N D E X

ABOUT THE AUTHOR

Skip Miller is president of M3 Learning, a Los Gatos, CA-based sales training firm established in 1996. Miller is a sought-after speaker and consultant, and is author of the award winning *ProActive Sales Management, ProActive Selling, Knock Your Socks Off Prospecting,* and *Ultimate Sales Tool Kit.* He has authored and implemented numerous American Management Association training programs, as well as M3's hugely successful Advanced Sales School. He has been featured in such publications as *The San Jose Mercury News, The Chicago Tribune, Dallas Morning News, Sales and Marketing Management, Selling Power, The American Salesman,* and *Entrepreneur Magazine* and is a regular guest on business talk radio.

As president of M3 Learning, Mr. Miller has provided sales and sales management training and has keynoted sales events to hundreds of companies worldwide. In addition, he has authored a host of M3 learning courseware offerings: *ProActive Sales Management*™, *ProActive Sales Management II*™, *Interviewing Hiring Salespeople*™; *ProActive Selling*™, *Value!*™, *ProActive Sales Strategies*™, *Negotiate!*™, *Present!*™, and *Selling to Power* ™.

An instructor for American Management Association (AMA) in the areas of sales, sales management, and sales force automation, he has also authored and advised on AMA training programs and is the chairperson for the AMA Sales Leadership Conference. Previously, Skip was a vice president for Dataquest, a leading high technology market research firm. He held numerous positions there, including General Manager-North America, Vice President for North American Sales, Marketing, Client Services, Direct Products, Conferences, and Vice President-Latin America. Before moving to the Bay Area, he was Vice President and General Manager of Dataquest Global Events (DGE), formerly known as the Invitational Computer Conferences (ICC) division. Dataquest's record revenue and earnings growth during Skip's tenure were unprecedented in its history.

Prior to Dataquest, Mr. Miller spent 11 years in the Computer-Aided Design/Computer-Aided Manufacturing (CAD/CAM) market with McDonnell Douglas, where he was involved in numerous sales, sales management, and marketing management positions. His experience in sales, marketing, and operational management spans 25 years.